JULIUS C

The Ill-Fated Cricketer

And the players of his time

Geoff Amey

For my grandchildren
Lisa, Sarah, Charlotte and Taylor

First published in Great Britain in 2000 by
BODYLINE BOOKS
150a Harbord Street, Fulham, London SW6 6PH

ISBN 0 9538387 0 6

Printed and bound in Great Britain by Clifford Frost Ltd,
Lyon Road, Windsor Avenue, London SW19 2SE

BY THE SAME AUTHOR:
The Collapse of the Dale Dyke Dam 1864
City Under Fire: the Bristol Riots and Aftermath

CONTENTS

Foreword

The west Surrey township of Godalming has been touched only lightly by the demolition and fumes and hustle and bustle of the modern age. If you direct your gaze towards the spire of the ancient parish church of St Peter and St Paul from where Meadrow, Farncombe meets Bridge Road, at the north-eastern end of the town, across meadows known as the Lammas land that line the River Wey, it is as if the 20th century still lies some way in the future. In the winding backstreets and even along the High Street, 'progress' has mercifully been resisted or restrained. Between the curious 'pepper-pot' building (1814) at one end and, at the other, the King's Arms & Royal (once visited by Peter the Great, the giant Czar of Russia, and also the setting for a welcome-home banquet for the Surrey cricketers after that pioneering voyage to North America in 1859) the frontages gently proclaim the accumulation of the years. The mark '1663' on the brickwork halfway along the street arrests strangers in their tracks. And which is the building where the chilling Chennell murders took place in 1817?

In Godalming, the spirit of James Oglethorpe, founder of the state of Georgia, surely abides; so too that of Gertrude Jekyll, writer, artist and renowned garden designer; and Jack Phillips, gallant chief wireless operator, lost in *Titanic*; and, of course, the tortured spirit of Julius Caesar, still the premier cricketer to have emerged from this quiet, neat, little town.

'Julie' lived from 1830 to 1878, which does not feel so very long ago as you wander down Mill Lane, past the splashing water-wheel, to where the old Railway Tavern (now converted to offices) abuts the railway station (opened in 1859). In a room in that hotel the shattered middle-aged cricketer endured the final phase of his life in gloom and disillusionment and conceivably something of an alcoholic haze. What tales he could have told about the cricket stars and lesser lights of the mid-Victorian period and their adventures up and down England and in North America, Australia and New Zealand.

With much lamentation, he was buried in Godalming's old cemetery, but without any memorial. That regrettable omission is being put right, well over a century later, and in the same year that this first full-length and long-overdue biography is published.

For many years, Geoff Amey worked exhaustively on this fascinating and recurringly tragic tale and its surrounding folklore. He found that

5

mainstream publishers had abandoned the handsome tradition of taking on an occasional book which would not be a big moneyspinner but which had a distinct charm and would add prestige to their lists. Geoff was disappointed, though sanguine about it. A friend pointed out to him that he was by no means alone in having suffered rejection by a publisher. After all, what do they know of publishing who worship only profit?

And to the rescue came young Giles Lyon, whose little company Bodyline Books had already made a considerable impact on cricket's connoisseurs and collectors. Calculations and estimates caused furrowed brows, but at last the green light for the resurrection of Julius Caesar of Godalming, Surrey and England gleamed.

Here was an attractive figure, a sportsman in the fullest sense, ever ready to laugh, with hints that he might have been one for the girls; married at the outrageous age of 20. Beyond all this, he was a bit of a genius with the cricket bat, an imperishable part of sports history not only from being a member of the elite Surrey and All-England teams of the 1850s and early 1860s but also through his participation in the momentous inaugural international cricket tour, across the stormy Atlantic in the autumn of 1859.

Personal tragedies came to crush him. Within a span of 17 years, the loss of an infant daughter and the premature death of his wife had been savagely compounded by the accidental shooting of a man and the suicide of Caesar's son. Disintegration of the soul was a drawn-out and cruel inevitability.

This book, though, is not by any means black-bordered throughout. The cricketer with the distracting name of a Roman emperor had fun, he charmed and amazed with his cricket skill, and, as Geoff Amey demonstrates, the era was teeming with interesting cricketers who shaped the game for better or worse. If it bore scant resemblance in many ways to the cricket we watch today, that does not mean it was inferior. And if Julius Caesar had only known it, for all his setbacks he was at least spared the attentions of the inquisitive media octopus which intrudes obsessively into today's society.

So Caesar emerges from the shadows at last. I think you will find his story absorbing. Meanwhile, all I can say to the author is, Geoffrey, I told you so.

DAVID FRITH

Guildford, March, 2000

Introduction

This is not another book about Julius Caesar. It is a book about another Julius Caesar, the 19th century cricketer whose success with the bat contrasted sharply with the tragedy of his personal life.

Caesar, a carpenter from the west Surrey town of Godalming, played a prominent role on the cricket stage between 1849 and 1867 - a period embracing important developments in the game. He appeared for his county and country and the famous travelling All-England XI, was a member of the first England team to go overseas (to Canada and the United States) in 1859, as well as being part of the 'flower of English cricketry' which toured Australia and New Zealand in 1864. Cricket in his day included colourful characters like William Lillywhite, Alfred Mynn, John Wisden, William Clarke, 'Mad Charlie' Brown, 'Foghorn' Jackson, George Parr, 'Tear-'Em' Tarrant and, latterly, an up-and-coming young man called William Gilbert Grace.

Like his 'noblest' Roman namesake, Julius Caesar lived in an era of commercial and social revolution. On the cricket field, too, there were rifts and recriminations leading, in the 1860s, to an 'uncivil' war between northern and southern players. And, during Caesar's lifespan (1830-1878), the game evolved from comparative obscurity to widespread acceptance and, not long after his death, to the so-called 'Golden Age'. Caesar typified the professional cricketer of his time. He was a popular sportsman. But a series of grievous misfortunes (bereavements and his accidental killing of a fellow townsman and then the suicide of his own 17-year-old son) reduced an erstwhile vibrant soul to a 'mere resemblance of his former self'.

In tracing the life of this renowned cricketer through the jovial halcyon years to its melancholy finale, the book also outlines the broader theme of cricket's expansion during the Victorian age and some of the fascinating personalities involved in it.

Anyone who gets to the end of this book without skipping pages deserves my thanks - none more so than David Frith (the founder of *Wisden Cricket Monthly*) for his generous encouragement from an early stage, for writing the foreword and organising the illustrations. I am also grateful to John Janaway and Duncan Mirylees, both of the former Surrey Local Studies Library at Guildford, for their cheerful assistance during my researches there. The match award goes to my wife, Jean, for her all-weather support and for being the serene inspiration of a long unbroken partnership.

GEOFF AMEY

Guildford, March 2000

Julius Caesar

Chapter One

The Town and the Boy

By the 1820s, Godalming had long been familiar to coach travellers as a staging point midway between London and Portsmouth. It was also well known in the summertime to followers of cricket as both a venue for important matches and for having a formidable club side of its own.

The small country town in south-west Surrey nestled in a verdant valley bounded by tree-studded hills, but those sylvan surroundings belied its bustling centre. Within a taut area were situated breweries, sawmills and tanneries, knitwear/hosiery manufacturers and papermakers, some half-a-dozen hostelries and a wide range of shopkeepers and tradesmen. A new public hall, built in 1814 and resembling a stone pepper-pot, stood at one end of the High Street. From the main thoroughfare wound lanes and alleys, and through meadows, not far away, meandered the River Wey along which horse-towed barges crawled to and from a little wharf. Bulky cargoes of sawn wood, flour and iron left for destinations en route to London and farther afield, while incoming goods included coal and grain.

Godalming was a comparatively prosperous and largely self-sufficient community of about 4000 souls into which had settled Benjamin Caesar, a young baker. It appears that he hailed from Peper Harow, a village some three miles to the west that, coincidentally, has its own niche in cricket history. About 70 years before his birth, the earliest known Articles of Agreement were drawn up for two matches there – in July and August 1727 – between teams raised by the Duke of Richmond and Alan Brodrick who, the following year, succeeded his father as Earl of Midleton.

Those written conditions, which were surely supplementary to a fuller code of rules no longer in existence, related directly to those two 12-a-side fixtures at Peper Harow Park, the Midleton family seat. Among other things, the Articles referred to umpires' duties, methods of dismissal and a pitch *23* yards long. (The oldest Laws of Cricket, dated 1744, specified 22 yards.)

Cricket, or at least the organisation of it, was then almost exclusively the preserve of the aristocracy and other rich landowners – just another pastime, like hunting and gaming, to enhance the social calendar and involving considerable wagers and side-bets. Estate workers and domestic servants were often retained also for their cricketing ability to be led into sporting battle against the forces of wealthy rival patrons. It is within the realms of possibility that a Caesar or two took part in those games at Peper Harow.

Ben Caesar subsequently became a useful local player himself, as did a number of his relatives. He got married by licence at Godalming Parish Church on November 3, 1816 to Ann Bowler. Less than four months later, it seems the young newly-weds again attended the church with the lofty spire by the river for another ceremony – the christening of their first child, George.

The even tenor of local life was seldom much disturbed, but it became rudely shattered by a double murder during the evening of November 10, 1817. It occurred close to where the Caesars lived and, in such a close-knit society, they would surely have known both victims and perpetrators. George Chennell, a 62-year-old shoemaker, and his elderly housekeeper, Elizabeth Wilson, were found in the living quarters behind his High Street shop. They had been battered, their throats cut and some valuables stolen. The old man's only son, George, and William Chalcraft, whom Chennell (senior) employed as a carter, were convicted at Guildford Assizes in August 1818 of the grisly crime, driven in an open cart to Godalming and hanged from gallows erected on the meadows before a crowd estimated at 20,000. It is probable Ben and his wife witnessed what transpired to be the town's last public execution.

Things gradually returned to normal and for Ben Caesar this meant baking bread for a living to provide for a growing family. The parish registers show that during the next decade, four more sons and a daughter of Ben and Ann Caesar were baptised at the church, each in the month of January: Richard (1819), Lawrence William (1821), Ann (1823), Benjamin (1825), and Frederick Bowler (1828: born October 11, 1827).

Another child, born on Thursday, March 25, 1830, was destined to achieve renown as a cricketer well outside the boundaries of Godalming and, indeed, far beyond the shores of Britain. On May 31, the Caesar family once more headed from their High Street home for the church and, gathered around the font, heard their latest addition christened 'Julius'.

He grew up in the atmosphere of cricket. Godalming was rated as one of the main centres of the county game and the Caesar clan boasted a battery of good local players, several of whom turned out under the banner of 'Surrey'. Julius's father, brothers, uncles and cousins participated in the sport or were to, with varying degrees of aptitude, and the family later fielded Twelve Caesars in a unique match with Eleven Gentlemen of Godalming and District.

Ben Caesar passed on his experience of bread-making to at least two of his sons, George and Fred. Indeed, George was in business as a baker and grocer from his early twenties and, it seems, ran a shop in the adjoining community of Farncombe for many years. Another son, Richard, became a butcher.

Fred was less enchanted with baking and, after a spell in that line, he had a complete change of heart, went to London and became a turnkey at Horsemonger Lane Gaol. Guarding prisoners did not appeal to him for long either and in 1860, when he was 33, he took over as mine host at a tavern in Southwark. Apart from Julius, brother Fred proved the most accomplished of the cricketing Caesars; he appeared for several club sides in south-west Surrey, occasionally played for the county and, in 1862, founded the New All-England X1 (albeit a short-lived venture). He was a licensed victualler in Bermondsey when death overtook him on October 5, 1882, leaving a personal estate of £5614 – then a handsome sum, especially in the eyes of most of the Caesars.

From earliest boyhood, Julius Caesar was immersed in local cricket lore. He must have heard of memorable matches staged at Godalming during the 1820s, when the town club fielded sides to defeat Sussex, Hampshire and even the powerful MCC. His father and uncles would have recalled with pride a golden occasion when Godalming was chosen as the venue for Surrey's duel with 'England' and also, with fervour, the bristly inter-town clashes between Godalming and Midhurst.

Exactly what young Julius received by way of conventional education is not possible to say but, almost certainly, he attended one of the two schools then established in the town. He could read and also write in a legible hand. Despite the obvious hardships of those times, an energetic lad could find much to enjoy. He would have been called upon to help with the household chores and, from an early age, to augment the family income but, when free from such duties, there was plenty else to do. He might visit the wharf perhaps, to watch the loading and unloading of hefty barges tethered to iron-ringed posts, or go into the High Street to see the strident arrival of stagecoaches.

There were also woods and fields to explore, a river and ponds to fish or, venturing outside the immediate vicinity, a journey to Guildford. According to William Cobbett, that indefatigable rider around rural England, there was 'hardly another pretty such four miles – the road is good; the soil is good; the houses are neat; the hills, the woods, the meadows, all are beautiful'. In addition, of course, there was cricket, with chances to see his relatives in action on the local grounds. Indeed, it would not be long before the boy himself would be proudly competing on equal terms in men's matches.

The young Julius quickly realised that cricket was no game for milksops; it was played with a ball that hurt when rearing wickedly from pitches often so rough that no self-respecting village club today would tolerate. Yet there were rewards for those prepared to challenge its ruggedness and of sufficient ability to vie with the sport's leading exponents: an opportunity to travel, the stimulus of exacting competition and public acclaim and, if one really made the grade, a measure of fame. Despite uncertain and irregular employment and a comparatively short career for modest remuneration, a professional cricketer could expect a healthier and more glamorous existence than most paid servants. Cricket provided nothing like a living year-round wage, of course, and a steady primary job was essential.

Although the precise origins of cricket lay buried in time immemorial, the south-west corner of Surrey had for long featured prominently in its history. The county town of Guildford, for instance, claims the first realistic recorded mention of the game. In 1598 coroner John Derrick, then 59 years old and testifying in a case about disputed land, recalled that when a pupil at the Free School (Royal Grammar School) 'he and diverse of his fellowes did runne and play at creckett and other plaies'. This puts the date at around 1550.

During the latter half of the 18th century, villages in the area produced some of the best players in the land that, in cricket geography, then virtually meant south-east England. Send-born Edward Stevens, for example, whose sobriquet of 'Lumpy' doubtless stemmed from his ample frame, was widely regarded at his peak as the foremost bowler and is credited with being mainly responsible for the introduction of the third stump following the tense finish of a five-a-side match at the Artillery Ground, London, in May 1775. The then premier batsman, John Small, got the 14 runs needed for victory, but not before missing several accurate deliveries from 'Lumpy' that passed through the two-stump wicket. It was considered such ill-luck that the laws were amended shortly afterwards.

Felix's 1851 watercolour of Caesar.

In that era there were, too, those 'anointed clod stumpers' – the Churt-born brothers, Tom and Harry Walker, raw-boned rustics whose family farmed land near the Devil's Punch Bowl at Thursley; the legendary batsman, William Beldham, and his brother-in-law, 'Honest John' Wells, both natives of Wrecclesham, near Farnham; and from Ash, some three miles away, came the powerful left-hand batsman, 'Long Bob' Robinson, who once arrived at the wicket in then unheard-of 'pads' – two thin boards set at an angle and attached to his right leg. Such was the merriment of fielders when the ball cracked against the guard, however, that poor Robinson was laughed out of his beloved brainchild. All those men appeared for the famous Hambledon (Hampshire) club, whose glorious exploits on Broadhalfpenny Down were so affectionately chronicled by John Nyren.

In terms of county cricket, Surrey remained virtually dormant during the 1820s and 1830s, with few matches of note. There was no overall administration or recognised focal point and the county's strength, albeit scattered, flourished in clubs like those at Godalming, Dorking, Montpelier, Reigate and Mitcham. During a purple patch in the 1820s Godalming, sometimes boosted by a 'given' man or two, could put out a side capable of beating the best. Regular stars during those halcyon days were William Searle and his cousin, the ill-fated James Saunders, both of whom played for Surrey, The Players and England.

The 'far-noted' Searle, who for a while kept the Three Lions Inn in Godalming, once hit 87 (then an unusually big score) for England at Lord's in July 1829 against a strong Sussex team which included the roundarm 'twins', William Lillywhite and James Broadbridge. On retiring from cricket, Searle became steward to a colonel at East Clandon, a village four miles north-east of Guildford, and was buried there on February 23, 1837, aged 41.

Although Searle's departure from the game was apparently voluntary, James Saunders, a Haslemere butcher, had no such choice. He contracted tuberculosis. A left-hand batsman of rare accomplishment, he recorded a number of large scores, including 156 not out for the Artillery Club against MCC in 1824 and 99 and 100 in 1825 and 1827 respectively for The Players. He prospered remarkably on rutted pitches and thick outfields, reaching a diamond peak in July 1824 by hitting 54, 63, 92, 156 not out and 39 consecutively – at an average of exactly 101 – an astonishing feat, especially at that time. It must have been harrowing to watch the consumptive corrosion of that sturdy young man. John Mitford, the cricket-loving editor of *The Gentleman's Magazine*, recalled seeing him when 'his cheek was hollow and his lips pale, but his execution was as fine as ever. His cut to point was unrivalled and his leg hit very powerful and sure'. Despite pain and despair, Saunders played on bravely until August 1831 and was but 29 when he died on March 27 the following year.

Julius Caesar would have been told of the affectionate esteem in which Saunders was held and also of the game in July 1820 when Godalming defeated by 28 runs near-neighbours Farnham, in whose team were 'Silver Billy' Beldham and John Wells, then aged 54 and 61 respectively. He would also have enjoyed the story of how, within the space of a month in 1824, Godalming beat both MCC and Sussex. The next season the town club, handsomely assisted by James Broadbridge, thrashed Hampshire by 202 runs and then dealt an even heavier blow to MCC by an innings.

So the town had been the colourful scene of major matches, hundreds of people from miles around arriving by coach, cart, on horseback and on foot to see the champions of the day in action. The rich and poor, the elegant and tattered, the graceful and graceless: all would make it a memorable day out. Tents were pitched, odds shouted, ale quaffed and meat pies munched. Such a festive occasion was that when Godalming was the venue for the game between England and Surrey in August 1829. The county eleven, aided by Lillywhite and Broadbridge as 'given' men, included a B.Caesar (it could have been Julius's father) and they won by four wickets.

For those encircling the green area, that encounter provided a rich feast. Towering above most of his England colleagues, both physically and socially, was William Ward MP, wealthy banker, generous patron of the game and a superb batsman with many fine scores already under his not inconsiderable belt. He was then 42, and nine years earlier had astounded the cricket world by hammering a hitherto undreamed-of 278 at Lord's for MCC against Norfolk. (It remained the highest individual recorded score until 1876 before being eclipsed, inevitably, by W.G.Grace, and the highest at Lord's for 105 years.)

Also in that England side was Thomas Beagley, the lanky Hampshire professional, who in 1821 became the first to make a century in the Gentlemen v Players series. Fuller Pilch, then regarded as the country's top batsman, was loudly applauded by the Godhelmians, but he was not fully fit and could manage only 4 in each innings. Even so, an admiring crowd glimpsed the regal style and matchless forward play for which he was renowned.

Surrey met a Kent XI at Godalming in September 1828, the latter winning by an innings and 42 runs, and an interesting sidelight was that a 'Caesar' appeared in each team. Sadly the scorer, blissfully unconcerned with posterity, failed to append initials. However, we do know that the Caesar playing for Surrey got a 'pair' while his namesake made the game's top score of 47. The young Julius doubtless knew the answer to that identity mystery, for he would have been keen to glean details about the town's cricket and, in particular, what his kinsmen had contributed.

Some time during the 1840s, it seems that Ben Caesar ran a bakery/grocery business in Bridge Street. Not far away dwelt William Brewser, a carpenter, his wife, Ann, and among their children, Jane (baptised July 26, 1829). She would one day be Julius's wife. Was it more than a coincidence that he also became a carpenter by trade?

In a grand house nearby and adjacent to the river bridge there resided, for a while at least, a well-heeled timber merchant. His public-school educated sons would play an important role in Julius Caesar's cricket career.

Chapter Two

Friends at Court

Julius Caesar's birth coincided with the dawn of the railway age. The rapid expansion of such revolutionary transport would offer increasing mobility to an erstwhile largely static population and, consequently, provide the means whereby top cricket, its star performers and more matches reached wider audiences.

Meanwhile, within the game itself, another revolution – that of roundarm bowling – had been smouldering for years. By 1830 its practice, if still illegal, was widespread. The credit for introducing this type of delivery has been popularly bestowed on John Willes, a well-to-do landowner, who lived at Sutton Valence in Kent. A keen amateur cricketer, he is reputed to have got the idea when his sister, bowling to him at their home, could not propel the ball underarm owing to the encumbrance of her crinolined dress. It might seem apocryphal, but is held to be true.

There was nothing fanciful about the hostile reception Willes and his emulators endured at some matches, however. Controversy intensified and, in 1816, MCC ruled the bowling action to be unlawful; but it did not stop. On the contrary, it grew and matters reached a fiery level at Lord's on July 15, 1822 when, playing for Kent against MCC, the persistent Mr Willes was promptly no-balled. It was the final straw for him. He stalked from the field 'in high dudgeon', leapt upon his horse, galloped from the scene and was seldom seen again on any ground of importance. He had left his mark, however.

By the middle of the 1820s, William Lillywhite and James Broadbridge especially were demonstrating just how effective the new style could be but, despite mounting pressure, the authorities declined to alter the law. A growing number of umpires, confused by the wording of the relevant clause and perhaps with more perception of the inevitable, tended to turn a benevolent blind eye to the rising elbow.

By literally elevating their bowling arm to a higher plane, Lillywhite and Broadbridge simultaneously hoisted Sussex to a fresh pinnacle and the county readily agreed to meet England in three 'experimental' matches in 1827 to test the relative merits of underarm and roundarm. Sussex won the first at Sheffield by seven wickets, those two bowlers recording 16 dismissals between them, and were also victorious in the second (at Lord's) by three wickets. At that point professionals in the England XI, including Pilch, Searle, Saunders and Beagley, refused to play the third unless their opponents 'bowl fair – that is abstain from throwing'. Unless it was some sort of orchestrated ploy or mere soreness in defeat, it is difficult to fathom, for surely the whole purpose of the series was to compare and assess the two types of bowling. In the event, the protest fizzled out and England went on to beat Sussex at Brighton by 24 runs.

The new style continued to attract additional exponents and converts every season and yet it was not until 1835 that MCC formally sanctioned what many players and co-operative umpires had unlawfully acknowledged for years. A similarly long-winded argument would rage later before overarm bowling was finally legalised in 1864.

During the 1830s and early 1840s – when Julius Caesar was a boy – most of the stars in the cricketing cosmos hailed from Kent, Sussex, Nottinghamshire and, to a lesser extent, from Yorkshire. Among them were Kent's Alfred Mynn, that kindly colossus who flourished on gigantic suppers and single-wicket victims, who proved himself to be the most eminent of all-rounders; his county colleague, Fuller Pilch, who gracefully reeled off a number of memorable innings; Sam Redgate, that 'very fast and ripping' Nottinghamshire bowler, who worked up a furious pace and with it an unquenchable thirst; Nottingham-born William Clarke, bricklayer and founder of the Trent Bridge ground, his best seasons yet to come, who confounded batsmen with innocuous-looking 'slows'; the incomparable William Lillywhite, self-confessed top bowler in the land; Thomas Marsden, the left-handed Sheffielder, who had once hit a double-century (227 in July 1826); James Dean, who learned the game from his village neighbours, those wide-shouldered Sussex farmer-brothers, James and William Broadbridge; and that refined run-maker from Nottingham, Joseph Guy.

Julius Caesar, who was to play alongside most of them, developed into a strong-limbed young man, albeit to a height of only 5ft 7in. Outward joviality would ensure he would not want for friends, although one gains the impression that his sometimes boisterous behaviour masked a nervous apprehension and sensitivity. He possessed considerable physical courage, showing a penchant for boxing, and was maybe a mite rough-hewn at the edges. Nevertheless, he took a pride in his personal appearance, dressing as neatly as finances permitted, could sink his share of pints with the lads, and, one suspects, his agreeable countenance and darkish hair appealed to the young ladies.

Unpretentious and congenial, Caesar mixed easily with people until a crop of tragedies in later life dragged him down. One might form a picture of a frank and friendly character, seemingly anxious to please and knowing his place, yet not without an aggressive streak and a dash of dogged independence. He appears to have been of a generally cheerful disposition that, nonetheless, could descend into troughs of dark depression. Few cricketers in his time would be better known or more popular with team-mates and crowds.

Caesar's name began appearing in newspaper reports of local matches when he was 16, but it is a sure bet that he started well before then. His brothers and cousins also turned out for the Godalming club which, compared with its present-day counterpart, had but a very small programme of fixtures. The town side that played Shillinglee in September 1846, for instance, included five Caesars (George, Benjamin, Richard, William and Frederick), though it is not possible to be certain of their relationship. (Shillinglee Park, the country seat of the Earl of Winterton, was just in Sussex, about eight miles south of Godalming.)

By no means the least of Julius's early mentors was Charles Woods, a stocking weaver by trade and for many years an outstanding bowler for Eashing whose home ground was adjacent to picturesque parkland very near Godalming. Woods was a shrewd campaigner whose slow deliveries had county class about them. As a young man of 21, he had been in the Surrey side at Lord's in June 1831 against a strong England XI whose line-up included Lillywhite and Beagley and the renowned amateurs, William Ward, E.H.Budd and E.G.Wenman. A suspect action was said to be the reason for his not appearing more often in important matches. Even when roundarm became legalised, Charlie's hand was considered to be 'too much up' – a nicety apparently overlooked by local umpires, and he went on collecting wickets until an old man. Woods was to outlive Caesar by seven years.

In addition to the valuable advice he received from Woods and other experienced players, Julius got encouragement from his father and brothers. He also needed an influential friend at court and he found several among the affluent Marshall family, whose aldermanic voices carried considerable weight not only in Godalming but, more significantly for an aspiring cricketer, at Kennington Oval.

Henry Marshall, a respected solicitor, was 41 when elected the town's first mayor in 1836 (there had been wardens prior to the Municipal Corporation Reform Act of 1835). He held office again in 1841-42 and was to serve further terms in 1853-54 and 1862-63. Of greater importance to this story, however, is that he was a prominent member of the newly-formed (1845) Surrey County Cricket Club, whose president he would be from 1856 until 1867.

His elder brother by six years, George Marshall, had inherited from their father the running of the family firm of timber merchants. In the process of effecting a marked business expansion, including the supply of English elm to the naval dockyards, he had enhanced his social and financial status. Sometime towards the end of the 1840s, George and his family moved from a Regency residence in Bridge Street to Broadwater House, an imposing mansion by a glinting lake, a mile along the road from Godalming to Guildford. Next to his home, he arranged to have laid out the 'noted cricket ground upon which all the matches of the neighbourhood are played'.

George Marshall's eldest son, Alexander, was a captain in the Surrey Militia; the two youngest, Frederick and Harry, were to follow full-time Army careers, while a fourth, Murray, would succeed his father as head of the family business. All were good amateur cricketers, participated in many local matches and, with the exception of Murray, occasionally played for the county during the 1850s. Alexander, a hefty six-footer, proved the best and even toured the country in the exalted ranks of the All-England XI for a while. He and Frederick, who would take over the presidential reins of Surrey CCC from his Uncle Henry in 1867, took a particularly keen interest in the cricketing progress of Julius Caesar. The Marshalls, then, possessed a vital key of entry to the Surrey club and, what is more important, were prepared to unlock the Oval door for a talented youngster.

So, from several sources, discerning eyes focussed upon Julius from the moment he started to show exceptional promise. Elder brother Fred also displayed good form, it being noted by the *Surrey Gazette* that in one game in 1847 the bowling of the Caesars was 'as usual, of a superior kind'. Spectators 'much admired' the batting of Julius who, it was accurately forecast, 'bids fair to become a first-class cricketer'.

During another match of similar vintage, 'the two juvenile Caesars of Godalming then went in and played very beautifully and made fifty before

A vivid depiction of Julius Caesar: John Corbet Anderson's lithograph, published 1858.

they were parted'. Fred stole the limelight on September 6, 1847 when Godalming contested Shillinglee. Bowling to the Earl of Winterton, he hit and killed a swallow that unwisely flew into the path of the ball. The downfall of His Lordship shortly afterwards was a family affair: 'ct J.Caesar bld F.Caesar 5'.

Members of the Surrey club had a splendid opportunity of assessing young Julius at close quarters in June 1848 when the side visited Eashing Park and narrowly defeated Godalming by 17 runs. Caesar got only 6 not out and 7, but he got them against an attack which included professionals Tom Sherman and George Brockwell and did enough to be underlined as a positive county prospect. The local sages nodded agreement, for they had known it all along. Indeed, two years earlier on July 7, 1846, the *Surrey Gazette* had reported:

A single-wicket match was played on the New Ground, Godalming, between Julius Caesar, a lad of 16 years of age, of the Godalming Cricket Club, and Mr C.Coomber, of Eashing. Caesar went in first and obtained five runs which, with one wide, made six. Coomber fetched three runs which, with three wides, made six. Caesar for his second innings got 49, and wides three, making a total with the first of 58. Coomber followed and, after 35 balls were delivered, obtained no run and scored only one wide, leaving Caesar the winner by 51. The lad promises to be as noted in the game of cricket as his ancient namesake was in the art of war. The Godalming club are ready to back him against any lad of his age in the County of Surrey.

Chapter Three

Young Professional

On a June day in 1849, just 10 weeks after his 19th birthday, Julius Caesar walked out to bat at The Oval. Upon the recommendation of Alexander Marshall, he was in the Players of Surrey XI facing a team of the county's gentlemen – a match arranged primarily to 'bring together the rising cricketing talent in different parts of Surrey'. Also on trial was 21-year-old William Caffyn from Reigate.

The Gentlemen included the Honourable Robert Grimston (later president of MCC) and N.Felix, one of the most gifted amateurs of his time. The versatile Felix, whose real name was Nicholas Wanostrocht and who was for many years a schoolmaster, brought a scholarly touch to his batting, which featured a delicate late-cut and a breathtaking cover-drive.

Both on and off the field, Felix was a notable all-rounder: inventor of the Catapulta, a mechanical bowling device based on the design of the Roman siege weapon; the originator of tubular-rubber batting gloves; an accomplished musician; a very fine painter of portraits, animals and landscapes. (He did a full-length picture of Caesar and presented it to Alexander Marshall in September 1851.) Although now 44 and past his sporting best, Felix continued to inspire respect and affection.

Twelve years his junior, Grimston had the reputation of being one of few to have dealt comfortably with the fastest deliveries of Alfred Mynn in his heyday. He reportedly used to carry two bats to the middle when the Kent giant appeared for the opposition, changing from the heavier to the lighter for the lesser bowlers.

When the Players began their reply to a total of 79 Caesar, due in at number three, had not long to wait. Sherman, who opened with Kingston-born James Chester, went to a catch without scoring and the young man from Godalming set off to face a varied, if not very hostile, attack. Caesar's dislike of pretension extended to his batting which, for most of his career, remained uncomplicated and exciting. Spurning too many subtleties, he concentrated on hitting the ball firmly. He was no crude rural slogger, however. His strokes, founded upon admirable footwork and timing, were skilfully executed.

Basically a front-foot player, he rarely missed a chance to drive and his small build belied the power of his shots. As he matured, Caesar curbed a natural impetuosity and could, if the occasion demanded, present a stubborn defence. Nevertheless, he was happiest and most effective when on the offensive. He was a mighty punisher of loose bowling.

During that Oval innings, he may have demonstrated the value of the pull, a stroke then by no means common. Despairing purists regarded it as little more than a rustic 'mow', but Caesar recognised the shot as a remunerative weapon in the batsman's armoury and was among the first to exploit it. He was, too, a fine fielder, although his throwing could be embarrassingly erratic.

In a brief report, *Bell's Life in London* observed that 'J.Caesar succeeded and obtained a score of 30'. It must have been about the last time he was referred to as 'J.Caesar'. Almost invariably thereafter in match scores and reports it would be 'Julius Caesar' – doubtless because of his historic name – whereas initials had usually to suffice for other players.

Julius had every reason to feel pleased with his showing on that high summer's day, his score being exceeded in the match only by Caffyn, who hit an eye-catching 46. George Beldham, great-nephew of the illustrious 'Silver Billy', was rather less contented – clean bowled for nought. In their second innings the Gentlemen, 87 in arrears, could muster only 94 and Sherman and Brockwell soon knocked off the runs needed to ensure a 10-wicket victory. Caesar even had a bowl, a subsequent rarity, and took three wickets. Among his victims was Felix who, having scored 5, was surprised by a stray straight ball from Julius whose short spell contained no fewer than 11 wides. For all that, the county club must have been satisfied with their latest 'signing'.

Summarising the views of the colts' performances, as expressed by the 'London critics', the *Surrey Standard* said this: 'Caesar is a fine steady bat, but without the flair and finish of Caffyn; neither is his bowling so good; but his fielding at point is extremely beautiful'.

That was not Caesar's debut at The Oval, however. Towards the end of the previous season, he had been in the Godalming side that mauled the Surrey club (Brockwell, Sherman and nine amateurs). In that game, he surely clinched his county chances by hitting a mainly professional attack for 67 and 46. Godalming, who totalled 161 and 192 for 5 before the home team (158 in their only innings) 'gave up', also included Julius's brother,

Fred, and a B.Caesar (either his father or a brother?) as well as Alexander and Frederick Marshall.

Surrey County Cricket Club had been officially inaugurated in 1845, with William Strahan as their first president. The Honourable Frederick Ponsonby (later Lord Bessborough) had embarked upon the first of his 50 years as a vice-president and William Denison was appointed acting secretary. Denison, a fair cricketer and better remembered for his book *Sketches of the Players* (1846), was a parliamentary and law reporter for *The Times*. As a bowler of lobs, he earned the good-natured tag of 'Stick-'Em-Up' Denison.

The story of the county club's birth really started a year earlier when Montpelier CC, forced to quit the Beehive ground at Walworth, secured a piece of land at Kennington owned by the Duchy of Cornwall (hence Surrey's crest of the Prince of Wales feathers). A lease was granted for the playing of cricket and Montpelier's president, W.Houghton, installed as the proprietor. By March 1845 the first of 10,000 blocks of turf, cut from Tooting Common, had been tamped down on the four-acre site.

Soon after their formation, Surrey engaged professionals George Brockwell and William Martingell. Born at Kingston-on-Thames in 1811, Brockwell was an experienced all-rounder and his deliveries frequently 'slow, twisting and very puzzling'. The 27-year-old Martingell, a burly individual proficient with both bat and ball, joined Surrey from Kent. Although a menacingly fast bowler, he lacked control over his run-up and was said to have been no-balled 'several hundreds of times'. He proved to be a rather restless man and, after a few seasons, returned to Kent, subsequently playing for a number of clubs and then holding coaching appointments at Eton and Bradfield College, Reading.

Surrey's fixtures and finances were scant during those initial years although, having been permitted to convert a house on the ground for their own use, members and players enjoyed relatively comfortable accommodation from the outset. The outfield was then infested with thistles and other weeds, sheep being brought in to act as 'mowers'; the pitch, while perhaps somewhat rough by today's standards, was level and apparently far superior to most of those elsewhere. John Burrup, an original promoter of the club, took over the duties of honorary secretary in 1848 and, in due course, was to demonstrate his resourcefulness in a crisis.

A carpenter, a barber and a bricklayer – in the persons of Julius Caesar, William Caffyn and Thomas Lockyer, who were outstandingly good prospects as young cricketers – joined the Surrey payroll in 1849. Caffyn was a splendid all-rounder with 'good judgement and an admirable eye' and Richard Daft, the great Nottinghamshire batsman, would write of him: 'If Surrey ever possessed a finer player, I never saw him'. He remained a star of the county side until 1863 and also played for the All-England XI, the United All-England XI, The Players and the first three England teams to go overseas. At the end of the tour of Australia in 1864 'The Surrey Pet', as Caffyn was called, opted to stay and spent seven years 'Down Under' dividing his time between being a player-coach and his bread-and-butter job of hairdressing.

Lockyer, a 22-year-old from Croydon, was as good a wicketkeeper yet to appear and soon acknowledged as just about the best of the generation. He arrived on the scene when protective equipment was still rudimentary, but with quick reflexes and capacious hands, described as resembling saucepans, displayed a rare aptitude for the task. Lockyer continued to play for his county until 1866 and, like Caesar and Caffyn, would be in the very first England team to tour abroad (Canada and the United States in 1859) and was also included in the 1864 party to go to Australasia.

Aided by such a talented trio, Surrey could field a formidable side and, with the prospect of growing membership and consequent cash, seemed poised to pull away from a series of teething troubles. There lingered an irritating fly in the Oval ointment, however, and it took the form of the ground's proprietor of all people. Discontented with the revenue from cricket, Houghton boosted income by staging walking matches and poultry shows, 'to the annoyance of the neighbourhood', and, as a result, caused 'much injury' to the Surrey club.

Nevertheless, he ignored appeals to desist and the controversy culminated in 1854 with the Duchy's refusal to renew his licence. Foreseeing an opportunity to oust the proprietor for good, secretary John Burrup persuaded the club committee to boycott the ground (indeed, Surrey played no matches at The Oval that season). The manoeuvre succeeded and before the end of the year Houghton's brother, who held the lease on mortgage, agreed to terms. A new lease was granted to the club in the trusteeship of Charles Hoare (treasurer, who had been the county skipper 1846-50), Alexander Marshall and Henry Mortimer. John Burrup, whose perspicacity and enterprise had won the day, relinquished the secretaryship in favour of his twin brother, William, who held the office from 1855 until 1872.

The Oval, Kennington, 1850, Caesar's home ground as a Surrey player.
Today the Hobbs Gates and much else has replaced this early structure.

Having surmounted the Houghton hurdle, Surrey's future would brighten impressively. In 1855, for instance, there were 230 members and an income of around £500; by 1861, the membership had topped the thousand mark with money rolling in at a rate of almost £2000 annually. During that period, a pavilion was erected and the task of scorers was much eased by the introduction of a covered 'cabin' on wheels, complete with telegraph.

All of which would affect Julius Caesar's career in the years ahead. In the meantime, he experienced his initial taste of inter-county cricket in a match of some note – Surrey's first meeting with Sussex for 19 years – at The Oval on July 28/29, 1849. It was in at the deep end for Caesar, who opened the innings and managed second-top score of 15 in a total of 79. An altogether low-scoring affair ended in victory for Surrey by 15 runs.

In his second innings, Julius had been caught off the bowling of John Wisden, the pocket-sized wonder from Brighton, only 5ft 4in tall and then in his 23rd year. Wisden, an exponent of medium-fast roundarm, would astonish even his most avid admirers the next season by *clean bowling* all 10 batsmen in an innings during the North v South clash at Lord's. It is odd to find that Wisden played *against* The South on that occasion, but he and Nottinghamshire's George Parr had newly acquired a ground at Leamington and 'he was therefore considered to be domiciled in the north'. A somewhat tenuous reason, one might think.

From one great bowler to another. At The Oval on August 6/7, 1849, Julius Caesar had his first confrontation on the field with the redoubtable William Clarke, founder of the highly-successful All-England XI, who was playing for England against Surrey with 'given' men in Thomas Box and William Hillyer. At 40, Box was a doyen among cricketers and a long-serving reliable wicketkeeper for Sussex, while Hillyer, of Kent, was an accurate bowler of medium pace whose run-up has been likened to the hurried dignity of a waiter anxious to deposit a pile of hot plates. (In 1845, he had become the first to take 200 wickets [208] in 'important' matches in a season, a record that stood for 25 years.)

The weather held fine, the ground looked in 'admirable order' and 19-year-old Julius, who opened with Brockwell, was soon 'hitting away in good style'. He was dismissed for 18 before Clarke came on to bowl but in his second knock Caesar was induced to move back by him and nudged his stumps after scoring only 2. Clarke took nine wickets in the match, seven of them in helping to rout Surrey in their second innings of only 44. Even so, his effort failed to prevent the county from winning by 31 runs, a victory made possible by Hillyer. He bowled without respite throughout both England innings to gain 13 wickets including those of Guy (twice), Parr, Pilch and Mynn – as elite a batting quartet then to be found in the country.

It is probable that even then Clarke recognised Caesar as a prospective candidate for his cricket circus. In fact, less than two years later, the young Godalming man would join that feted band of travelling celebrities. Like the Marshall family, Clarke became a major factor in Julius's career, and it is more than likely that Alexander Marshall recommended him.

However one views William Clarke – acute businessman, dogmatic leader, perceptive tactician or unrivalled slow underhand bowler – he comes through as a remarkable, if rather tetchy, character. Although his prowess from an early age had been well known, he remained virtually unrecognised at any representative national level until his mid-forties. Perhaps it had something to do with his awkward temperament and predilection for plain speaking. The hierarchy would not have appreciated that.

In 1846, Clarke embarked upon an enterprise that ensured for him a place in sporting history. He introduced his touring All-England XI, taking class cricket and its top-of-the-bill artists to many parts of Britain mainly to tackle local sides of up to 22 players. The public, especially those in remote areas, loved it – a sentiment not always shared by county cricket clubs, some of whose star performers stayed under 'contract' to Clarke for several weeks at the beginning and end of each season. Inevitably, there were fixture difficulties and team-selection clashes, but overall the AEE did a great deal for the game.

Between 1847 and 1853, according to one estimate, Clarke obtained a staggering total of 2385 wickets, including 476 in 1853, by which time he was in his 55th year. It has been pointed out, of course, that many of his victims were fourth-raters and, rather unkindly perhaps, that as self-appointed captain of the AEE, he made sure of doing plenty of bowling at the right time. If that is so, it is also true that few, if any, top batsmen ever really mastered him either. He was able subtly to vary his pace, length and direction and also *thought out* many of his adversaries. An accident at fives during his twenties cost Clarke the sight of his right eye, a disability that seems not unduly to have impaired his cricket.

Compared with the AEE's hectic excursions, Caesar completed the 1849 season in quiet fashion. On August 20 he played for Godalming, who defeated Brighton by 30 runs, being run out for a duck in a mix-up with brother Fred. He was back at The Oval a month later for a three-day 'repeat' of Surrey Players against Twenty Gentlemen of Surrey Club, the former winning by two wickets. Caesar reached 25 in his second innings before being bowled by the 21-year-old all-rounder Frederick Peel Miller, under whose exacting captaincy between 1851 and 1857 the county were to win 24 and draw three of their 35 major matches. (Charles Alcock, Surrey secretary 1872-1907 and founder-editor of *Cricket,* declared that Miller's methods 'may have been a little lacking in the sweet reasonableness which makes an ideal captain, but this was due to an excess of zeal than to any natural defect'.)

At the middle of the 19th century protective gear appears not to have attracted universal usage partly, one suspects, because of its limited quality but also because some players simply deigned to go to the middle anyway clad in such appendages. It was almost as if a painful blow ought to be stoically endured and bruises to be honourably worn like medals. A few batsmen, declining to attach leg-protectors for all to see, compromised by shoving a sort of shin-guard into their socks. Fashions and laws were quickly changing, however. Boundaries were the exception rather than the accepted rule until the 1860s, so that all runs had to be run, and an over comprised four balls until 1889, when it was increased to five.

Trousers were normally white, albeit a rather grubby off-white, but shirts were of various hues and patterns. Richard Daft said that 'the neatest of coloured shirts I recollect were those of our All-England Eleven, which were white with a small red spot or, sometimes, white with a narrow red stripe'. Boots had by now superseded shoes, while headgear underwent a series of modes – tall, top, billycock and velvet – leading to precursors of the sort of caps familiar today. Felix, who paid close attention to cricket apparel, recommended a cap of chequered woollen because it was 'light and cool to the head, absorbs perspiration and (what is not an insignificant fact) is not likely to blow off and hit the wicket'.

Although it is difficult to pin down precisely, the going rate for a professional around 1850 seems to have averaged about £4 for a match lost or drawn and approximately £5 for a win. An incentive bonus of a sovereign existed at some clubs for a batsman scoring a half-century and, in exceptional cases, he might get a share of a special ground collection. Similar carrots for bowlers appear to have been rarer. A good player could anticipate, though not be certain of, a benefit match or two and there was extra money to be derived from coaching at the universities and public schools. It should be remembered, however, that travelling expenses were seldom reimbursed for the many miles covered during a season.

Cricket nevertheless offered an absorbing life while it lasted and Julius Caesar, back at his carpenter's bench, doubtless reflected happily on his entry into the upper echelons of the game. Godalming remained much the same: stagecoaches continued to clatter along the High Street, the harvest was stored, autumn's chill arrived as did the first trains along the extended line from Guildford, late leaves floated down from the trees and the busy little town, set amid guardian hills, prepared for winter. Then springtime and another cricket season.

Chapter Four

Family Honour

Astocky old man, dressed in a tall hat, high-collared shirt and black tie with conspicuous braces hoisting up tightly-trimmed trousers, ambled to the wicket and, as he had done many a thousand times, sent down a ball of tantalising length. At the far crease, making his first appearance at Lord's, stood Julius Caesar, for whom the special moment was perhaps tinged with some regret at not having faced the 'Nonpareil' at his zenith.

On that May day in 1850 there lingered nostalgic tell-tale signs that William Lillywhite, then nearly 59, had been one of the greatest if not the greatest of all roundarm bowlers. The economy of effort, smooth medium delivery, accurate pitch and seemingly tireless application were still in evidence – indelible hallmarks of long dedication. Some of the snap, twist and lift may have vanished with the years, but here was a sight to savour: an exciting glimpse of the master craftsman at work.

Lillywhite, only 5ft 4in tall, had a rubicund face and behind his 'most kindly expression' lurked a determination, or bloody-mindedness, not easily shaken. Even now, his bowling was not to be trifled with. Nor was he. Yet the degree of benign respect felt for 'Old Lilly', faults and all, approached veneration. More than five summers had passed since the brightly fading little giant left his native Sussex to live in London, and on this occasion he was playing for Middlesex against Surrey.

Off the field, Lillywhite might permit himself a quip or two, but out there in the middle life was earnest. The finest cricket, he once confessed with disarming honesty, consisted of 'me bowling, Pilch batting and Box keeping wicket'. He had no reservations about his own ability. 'I bowls the best ball in England,' he used to say – an assertion that went largely unchallenged except, possibly, by a strict grammarian. If a batsman had the temerity to hit the ball back over his head, an offended Lillywhite would mutter: 'That's a pretty game, but it ain't cricket.'

His former bowling ally, James Broadbridge, who first graced Lord's as far back as 1817 when Surrey-born William Lambert became the first to score two centuries in a match, had died in February 1843, aged 47.

Lillywhite survived 'Our Jem' to take hundreds more wickets and was to continue playing, and coaching the boys at Winchester College, almost until cholera killed him on August 21, 1854. (A monument in Highgate Cemetery was erected on behalf of MCC members and friends, an inscription including the lines: 'Rarely has man achieved more applause in his vocation – few have ministered to more happy hours'.) Here, then, was the living legend bowling to young Julius, who managed to escape the veteran's wiles to score 13 and 22 not out in Surrey's nine-wicket victory.

A fortnight after his debut at Lord's, Caesar made another important appearance – this time in front of the altar. It probably came as no surprise to friends that he got married to Miss Jane Brewser, but there is reason to suppose that Guildford was used as a kind of Gretna Green. Bride and bridegroom, both natives of Godalming, gave the same address of Stoke Fields (Guildford) and, perhaps more significantly, their ages as 22. In truth each was only 20 when the curate, the Revd William H.Stevens, pronounced them man and wife inside the parish church of Stoke-next-Guildford on Tuesday, June 4, 1850.

One might speculate. Was there some family friction or a lack of parental consent, so prompting the couple to move to Stoke Fields for residential qualification and the calling of banns? In that same place lived Charles Caesar, aged 24, a railwayman (maybe a cousin); perhaps the 'runaways', if indeed they were, stayed temporarily with him and his wife, Harriet. Nearby dwelt Robert Stickland, a 32-year-old tailor, and a witness at the wedding. It throws no real light on just why the ceremony took place outside Godalming, however.

Be all that as it may, the most feasible explanation influencing the decision seems to have concerned a 'third party' – a son, subsequently born on July 29. When a census enumerator called at their home in Meadrow, Farncombe, the following March, the Caesars returned their then correct ages as 21 and that of the only other family occupant as eight months. (The birth certificate records the boy as Frederick William, but it was with the forenames of Frederick Sankey that he was christened at St John's Church, Farncombe, on December 1, 1850.)

Within two days of the wedding, Caesar was back at The Oval helping his county to defeat Middlesex again. He also played there a month later when Surrey met Kent for the first time in three seasons and recorded another easy win, by an innings and 110 runs. They totalled 246, Brockwell and Chester each making a half-century and Caesar a breezy 36 against an attack in which no fewer than 10 bowlers were tried. Among them was Edmund Hinkly, a left-arm paceman, who had burst into prominence during his debut at Lord's two years earlier by taking all of England's second-innings wickets to add to his six in the first. Surrey batsmen also had to contend with Edgar Willsher, of whom Caffyn said it was 'almost impossible to speak too highly'. The left-arm Kent bowler, then 21, had 'an extraordinary command' over the ball, which he could whip across from leg to off most effectively.

At the end of July, Caesar rubbed shoulders with several of the 'greats' when the All-England XI attracted a big crowd to watch them at odds with Fourteen of Surrey. Clarke's tourists scored 119, eight of their wickets falling to publican Daniel Day, a nippy bowler with a high delivery point, who claimed five more in the AEE's second innings of 84 after Surrey had made 115 in a drawn game. Caesar was bowled for 18 by Clarke, who possessed an uncanny knack of sizing up the opposition. He tended to treat gentlemen with a kind of deferential disdain and might greet an incoming batsman with: 'Beg pardon, sir, but ain't you from 'Arrow? Then we shan't want a player down there', ordering a fielder to 'stand for the 'Arrow drive between point and middle wicket'.

While the star-studded Clarke contingent roamed the Midlands, taking new-recruit Caffyn with them, Julius Caesar participated in a unique match. Hundreds of Godhelmians wended their way to the Broadwater ground beside the lake on the morning of Thursday, August 8, 1850, for the opening of a two-day match between Twelve Caesars and Eleven Gentlemen of Godalming and District. For weeks the forthcoming encounter had been a talking point over pots of ale in hostelries, local pundits working themselves into a lather, and consequently more thirst, debating the merits of the teams. A deal of money rested on the outcome, and odds, mainly favouring the Caesars, fluctuated sharply before and during the contest.

Family honour was entrusted to Julius, his father, three brothers, three uncles and four cousins. (Another source suggests their line-up included four brothers and two uncles. It is impossible to be certain because so many Caesars had the same forenames, but the former combination seems the more likely.)

Rain interrupted play several times on the first day, but as the game built up to a climax on the second a vast crowd encircled the arena and, reported *Bell's Life*, 'lovers of cricket have seldom had a greater treat'. Alexander

31

Marshall, son of the ground's owner, struck the highest score of the match, his 47 not out being compiled 'in beautiful style' in the Gentlemen's first innings of 123. That the Caesar clan replied with 95 was due largely to an eighth-wicket partnership between Richard, who got 20, and brother Fred with 19.

The 'Esquires' were shot out for 42 in their second innings, leaving the Caesars to get 71 to win, and they were heavily backed at three-to-two to do so. Much to the surprise of the enthralled onlookers and to the distinct displeasure of the punters among them, the family failed to make more than 54, Julius emerging as top scorer with 11. It was victory for the Gentlemen by 16 runs. Most of the Caesars' bowling had been done by Fred (11 wickets) and Julius (six) but their father, then in his mid-fifties and not to be denied, helped by taking one wicket and holding two catches. Despite their defeat, the Caesars were warmly praised for such a good showing against the best amateurs in the area (some of county standard) and they received 'substantial testimonials'.

On September 14, also at Broadwater, family honour was again at stake – this time in a single-wicket contest between Three Caesars (Julius, Fred and William) and Three Walkers (John, Frederick and Alfred). Like the Caesars, the Walkers of Southgate were members of a large and redoubtable cricketing family that, in their case, produced some of the finest amateurs of the era. Frederick Walker, for example, was destined to hit 157 for Southgate against Surrey in a little over three hours. His six brothers were also to shine in the first-class game, none more brilliantly than Vyell Edward Walker, to whom would come the glory of taking all 10 wickets in an innings and scoring an undefeated century in the same match at The Oval in 1859. 'V.E.' blossomed into 'one of the best all-round cricketers who ever donned flannels' – a tribute from a professional.

At least the Caesars did not have to contend with 'V.E.' (as yet, aged only 13), but they had plenty on their hands. It proved a dour struggle. Although only 51 runs were recorded in an 'unfinished' game, the finale contained enough excitement to make it all worthwhile. (The laws for single-wicket matches dictated that a batsman, with one foot grounded behind the popping crease, could score only when hitting the ball in front of the wicket. A 'run' entailed getting to the bowler's end and back – two normal runs to count a single. In games involving fewer than five players a side, neither byes nor overthrows were credited.)

The Caesars were dismissed for 8 and the hefty Walkers, all bowled by Julius, replied with 6. In their second innings the Godalming trio, or more accurately Julius on his own, totalled 18. When stumps were drawn, John Walker had made 18 and needed just two more to clinch victory. His brothers, who mustered a solitary run between them, had again been clean bowled by Julius. Indeed, for the youngest Caesar, not yet 21, that game marked a personal high note on which to complete the season.

A much heralded event in 1851 (the year of that other Great Exhibition in Hyde Park three miles away) was the first-ever encounter between Surrey and Nottinghamshire, which drew an unusually large crowd to The Oval on July 17 and 18.

Although without Cris Tinley, their 20-year-old fast bowler who later changed with far more success to 'slows', the Midland county paraded a splendid array of talent. George Parr, a blue-eyed, ginger-whiskered, independent man of 25 and dubbed 'The Lion of the North', was widely regarded as the best batsman around. His elder brother Samuel turned out, as did their unrelated namesake, Butler Parr. The team also included sophisticated stroke-maker Joseph Guy, said to possess elegance enough to play before Queen Victoria in the royal drawing-room; velvet-capped James Grundy, a 27-year-old grocer, whose best bowling was reputedly so accurate that he could 'keep dropping'em on a cheese plate'; evergreen William Clarke and his son, Alfred, a 'very good all-round man'; Frank Tinley, elder brother of Cris; and Thomas Nixon who, though in his 42nd year, had lost little of his guile as a slow bowler.

Surrey, captained by C.H.Hoare (deputising for F.P.Miller), also fielded a powerful eleven and had recently recruited a notable future mainstay in William Mortlock, a promising fresh-faced batsman of 18. The match offered a fascinating chance to compare the respective skills of wicketkeepers Tom Lockyer and 'Mad Charlie' Brown, a Nottingham dyer of excitable temperament, whose party-piece was to bowl the ball from behind his back.

The strapping Lockyer, who often sported a flannel waistcoat which Caesar impishly suggested had come out of the Ark, seldom failed to impress with his positive handling, particularly on the leg side. Although not quite in the same class, perhaps, Brown was 'as quick as lightning and as clever as a monkey' and apparently not averse to a spot of sharp practice. It seems that 'Mad Charlie' had been known to deceive batsmen and umpires alike by nipping off a bail when the ball passed close to the stumps and, moreover, conveniently refraining from mentioning the fact.

For Caesar, whose current form augured well, the keenly anticipated game assumed nightmare proportions. He was twice out without scoring and became 'extremely dejected'. A fear that any batting failure would lead to his immediate dismissal from the side haunted him throughout his career.

While he pondered and fretted over how Nixon had dollied him out, Chester and Caffyn were mainly responsible for steering Surrey to a first-innings total of 121. Contrary to general expectations, Nottinghamshire fell apart for 48. Guy went for 0, Parr for 1, and but for stout resistance by Samuel Parr and Brown, the collapse would have been even worse. The home side then scored 106, leaving Notts to get 180 for victory. They failed to do so and Surrey won the first of many Olympian battles between the counties by 75 runs.

Only three days after that titanic struggle, Surrey visited Sheffield for another 'first' – this time against Yorkshire, who had recently emerged as formidable contenders. The northerners included George Chatterton, an accomplished wicketkeeper and hard hitter; fellow Sheffielder Henry Wright, a batsman of considerable polish; 31-year-old Thomas Hunt, scientific opener who also excelled in single-wicket duels (his life would end tragically in 1858 when he was run down by a train close to Rochdale station); and the popular 25-year-old George Anderson, a fine batsman. The match was staged on the Hyde Park Ground (the one at Bramall Lane opened four years later), Surrey winning by 72 runs. In the return game at The Oval at the beginning of August, Surrey were again successful (by 10 wickets), and so was Caesar, who recorded his maiden half-century (51) for the county.

Chapter Five

With the All-England XI

During the summer of 1851, Julius Caesar joined the All-England XI and played his first game for them in August at Newark. At only 21 years of age, he became part of a scintillating galaxy that radiated stars like Mynn, George Parr, Grundy, Wisden, Box and Hillyer. For his part, William Clarke had signed up something of a crowd-puller – a youngster of high potential and bearing an attractive box-office name.

Although scoring only 13 and 2, Caesar did somewhat better than did most of his new team-mates, and the AEE tasted rare defeat. They went down by 15 runs to Twenty-Two of Newark and District or, more realistically, to two of the three Tinley brothers; Cris, known to his friends as 'Spider', hit 50 and Frank 39, in their side's first innings of 135, and they then proceeded, with a little help from brother Vincent, to take most of the visitors' wickets.

Despite this hiccup, Clarke's men had rapidly asserted their superiority over nearly all opposition since first taking to the road five years earlier. By 1851, his biggest discernible headache seemed to be the impossibility of accepting the invitations and challenges which flooded in; but behind the scenes there were rumblings of discontent among players over appearance money.

Most matches were massively supported, spectators travelling many miles to gaze upon the cricket giants and, as occurred occasionally, to cheer a home win. The leading citizens of each town vied with their counterparts elsewhere in planning the grandest welcome, most liberal hospitality and also the largest 'gate' receipts, which, in particular, would practically guarantee a return visit the following season.

As well as being memorable for the cricket, those occasions had something of a carnival atmosphere about them. Such festivities made a pleasantly enduring impression on Richard Daft, who recalled: 'One never sees such holiday-making and high jinks as we used to do in the old All-England days, especially at those matches played in small country towns. The All-England match was a topic of conversation months before the event took place. Special committees were formed to get up entertainment in the evening and, when the great day arrived, the excitement was often intense.' Although facing far greater numerical odds, the AEE were usually much too good for the local team, and to make a game of it the resourceful Clarke sometimes 'lent' the opposition one or two of his own men. Such a policy had to be calculated carefully because of cricket's uncertainty, as a string of defeats for the tourists would undoubtedly diminish their magnetic appeal.

Clarke and his band proceeded feverishly from one venue to another, snatching sleep when they could. Although the fast-expanding railway network went so far, it was frequently necessary to journey by spine-jarring coach. Felix recounted that once when the AEE travelled overnight by horse-drawn omnibus from Lynn to Sleaford, the driver got hopelessly lost on the wastes of Holbeach Marsh. The party eventually came upon a crossroads, where Hillyer jumped from the vehicle and shinned up a signpost. He could make out no directions in the darkness, however, and descended rather more quickly than he had intended when Caesar and Caffyn, who were supporting him aloft, 'suddenly withdrew their prop and down fell the Lucifer of bowlers'. Tired, aching and bedraggled, the team finally reached their destination at five o'clock on the morning of their match.

Sadly, growing friction between Clarke and some of the players began to mar the tours, his aloof, penny-pinching attitude being the root cause. Although no evangelist motivated by pure altruism in spreading the gospel of cricket, Clarke nevertheless loved the game and also saw in it a chance to effect a handsome personal profit, but he was accused of grabbing too large a slice of the financial cake. As determined by Clarke, of course, players variously received between £4 and £6, out of which they had to pay expenses. The main dissatisfaction, it seems, was that wages remained static and far from reflected the rising revenue derived from an expanding programme.

In 1851, for instance, the AEE fulfilled some 35 fixtures, the last 14 of which, at the end of the season, were crammed into an eight-week period and included visits to places as far apart as Edinburgh, Devonshire and Brighton. It must have put a big strain upon the players and especially Clarke, then in his 53rd year and responsible for the organisation. Almost certainly, he was a bit of a Scrooge but he met no Marley's ghost to effect a conversion and, like most managing directors, believed himself to be worth every penny.

Julius Caesar failed to find much form as the AEE whistle-stopped across Britain, which probably plunged him into a murky depression, a melancholy aspect of his otherwise bright temperament. He also had a strange nervous fixation about sleeping in hotels, fearing a previous occupant had died in the bed or that the building was about to be burned to the ground. Caffyn recalled how 'Julie' would awaken him in the middle of the night, worried lest the place be alight. Once, when they shared a room in Hereford, the yells of a drunkard could be heard from outside. Quite convinced there was a fire and getting no response from Caffyn, Caesar rang the alarm bell. Bewildered guests, clad in night attire, rushed about in all directions until they were rounded up and pacified by the red-faced proprietor.

Despite his phobias, Caesar was among the liveliest and most popular members of the AEE, ever ready with piquant repartee and a willing party to practical jokes. Sometimes he became the butt. He toured with a portmanteau and, like George Parr and his hat-box, valued it highly. He made a point of extolling its superior leather construction but the article was plainly too commodious for his requirements and, with other baggage piled upon it, the prized possession got squashed as 'flat as a pancake'. He occasionally had difficulty in locating it at all, much to the undisguised delight of his companions.

The AEE programme continued well into October that season, the final call being at Hove, where they drew with Sixteen of Sussex. Caesar felt much better after making the game's top score of 35. An interesting inclusion in the home side was Frederick Lillywhite, a son of William and the younger brother of James and John. Although he 'did not set himself up as a cricketer', Fred took part in notable matches from time to time, but far more often attended in his capacity as a newspaper reporter. He pioneered the production of up-to-date scorecards during play, his tent and printing press being a familiar sight at grounds. Fred also published a number of cricket books and was in partnership for a while with Wisden in a sports shop near Leicester Square, London. He seems to have been a controversial and rather fastidious young man, albeit industrious and enterprising, and packed a lot into his short life, which ended in 1866 when he was only 37.

Smouldering resentment within the rebel ranks of the All-England XI at last burst into open flame. Instead of attempting to alleviate the situation, however, Clarke adopted his customary remoteness. Some members thereupon broke away to form a rival team. The secession was headed by

Wisden and his Sussex colleague, James Dean, who became joint secretaries of the United All-England XI launched in the late summer of 1852. Dean, a plump man of 36 with downland air in his cheeks, supplemented his fast roundarm bowling with some circumspect batting. He gained the nickname of 'The Ploughboy'. In fact, he was a sawyer.

Lockyer, Chatterton, Nixon and Grundy were among others who could stand no more of Clarke's parsimony and martinet manner, and the United also recruited John Lillywhite, Sherman and Yorkshire's John Berry. The next season, Martingell defected to the United, who, in 1855, were to be joined by Caffyn. Much grievance undoubtedly existed but, having seen the huge success of Clarke's venture, Wisden and Dean and their fellow departees were surely also spurred on by the realisation that there was room and profit enough for two touring outfits.

The United All-England XI commenced their programme encouragingly at Daniel Day's ground in Portsmouth at the end of August 1852, defeating Twenty Gentlemen of Hampshire (with Day) by eight wickets. Ten days later, during a game at Sheffield, the United members gathered at their hotel to append signatures to a strongly-worded document. It declared that none of them would 'at any time play in any match of cricket, for or against, wherein William Clarke may have the management or control (county matches excepted) in consequence of the treatment they have received from him at Newmarket and elsewhere'. Precisely what happened there was unspecified (most likely it concerned Clarke's adamant refusal to a final request for more money), but no doubt remained as to the earnestness of the 14 players who signed that uncompromising statement.

So the touring sides went their separate ways. Predictably, it was not long before there arose a clamour from the public to see a grand match between them. The time was clearly not conducive, however, the air still being highly charged with an amalgam of animosity and recrimination. An infuriated Clarke flatly refused to entertain any suggestion of such a confrontation, while those of the UAEE who had committed themselves in writing were certainly not going to retract their stipulation about his management. (Not until after Clarke's death in 1856 did the public get their way.)

Caesar, the youngest in the AEE, remained with Clarke. So did Parr and Guy, who were both Nottinghamshire men, of course, as well as elder statesmen like Mynn, Felix, Box and Hillyer. One wonders how much Julius was influenced by his benefactor, Alexander Marshall, himself a pro-Clarke man. In a *Cricket Song for the Eleven of England*, composed in 1852 and signed 'A.M. Godalming', the last of five lyrical verses opened:

And long may 'Old Clarke' be up to the mark,
And guide us to triumphs again;
We shall never see better leader than he,
We may look for his like in vain.

In June that year, the All-England XI played on the Marshalls' trimly-cut Broadwater ground in a three-day match with Sixteen of Godalming and District for the financial benefit of Caesar, Martingell and Caffyn. If, as reported, the arena was in 'splendid condition, as level as a billiards table', it is surprising that the game produced only 181 runs for the loss of 49 wickets. The three beneficiaries turned out for the Godalming side, which also included four other Caesars (Frederick, William, Richard and John), two Marshalls (Alexander and Harry), George Beldham and Charlie Woods. The AEE, for whom Clarke took 18 wickets, won by a three-wicket margin, but not before Woods had demonstrated his class by clean bowling Guy, Box, Felix, Mynn and Grundy.

The most exciting happening, however, was the presence during the match of a cricketing colossus from the past – the legendary 'Silver Billy' Beldham, an ageless wonder of 86, who had walked from his cottage overlooking the village green at Tilford seven miles away. It is possible that Julius Caesar was related, albeit indirectly, to the old man. Living with Beldham at that time was his son-in-law, William Caesar, the 42-year-old local blacksmith. As five Caesars (including a William) and his own great-nephew, George, were playing in that game, Beldham could have been inspired to undertake the strenuous hike not only to watch the cricket but also to be part of a family reunion.

Be that as it may, the ancient figure with flowing white hair, dressed in a spotless smock and wearing a tall hat, stood erect, while his eye and speech had been but little impaired over the years. (Beldham had appeared in his last important match more than three decades earlier, when he was 55, for The Players against The Gentlemen at Lord's in July 1821. In that game, which also commemorated the coronation of George IV, he bade farewell with 23 not out.)

Beldham was warmly greeted at Broadwater by young and old alike in the crowd, anxious to shake the hand of the former master batsman. What tales he could tell of the characters who roamed the cricket circuit during the late 18th century, of those far-off days of the Hambledon club, drawing colourful images from the rich treasure-trove of his memory.

'Silver Billy' would live another 10 years before surrendering to the 'decay of nature'.

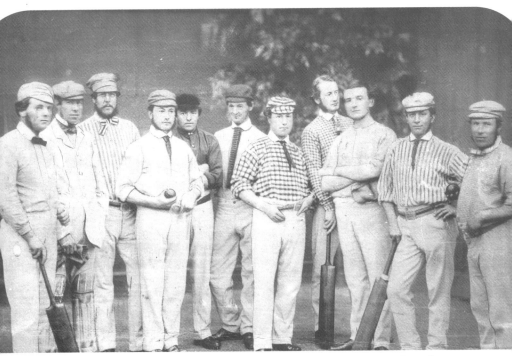

DAVID FRITH COLLECTION

The strong Surrey team of 1861: Billy Mortlock, Tom Lockyer, H. H. Stephenson, Billy Caffyn, George Griffith, Edward Dowson, F. P. Miller, C. G. Lane, Fred Burbidge, Julius Caesar, Tom Sewell junior.

Chapter Six

A Century and a Censure

From the moment he entered the realms of cricket's upper stratum, Julius Caesar seems to have been highly regarded by players and spectators. He was often called upon to open the innings, particularly in his early years, and, despite an inherent fear of failure, displayed a penchant for the task. Crowds thrilled to the batting of this young man with the emperor-like name. 'His hitting,' Richard Daft would write, 'was as smart and clean as anything that could be witnessed.'

The season of 1853 marked another milestone in Caesar's career. Still only 23, he made his first appearance for England and his debut was auspicious if only because it was tinged with controversy. The game was against Nottinghamshire at Lord's and his dismissal in the second innings occurred in an unfortunate way. Having made 7, he dabbed down on a sharp delivery from John Bickley and the ball spun towards the wicketkeeper who, in attempting to gather it, knocked off a bail. The umpire at the bowler's end, who may well have been unsighted, pronounced Caesar 'bowled'. The keeper, none other than 'Mad Charlie' Brown, and nearby fielders remained silent. Caesar walked.

Bell's Life in London commented: 'We should have thought that the other umpire ought to have been appealed to, and Caesar should have done so before leaving the wicket.' It is likely, however, that Julius himself was unaware at the time exactly what had happened. As England, needing only 75 to win, were ousted for 48 (Bickley 8 for 23), the decision proved to be somewhat crucial.

During the next few weeks, Caesar felt altogether happier. For the AEE he hit 20 and 63 not out at Cirencester, 48 at Wisbech and held six catches at Sleaford, where George Parr, who made 64, was given out 'hat fell on wicket'.

Caesar was again in the England team at Lord's in June, this time for an agreeable event of some note: a valedictory benefit match for William Lillywhite. Many of the leading players turned out to honour the 61-year-old. The national XI was opposed to Sussex (with Parr), Lillywhite playing for his native county alongside his sons, James and John, as well as Box, Wisden and Dean. Among those in the England team were William Clarke, who did not organise the match, of course, Grundy, Guy, Caffyn, Lockyer and Hillyer.

As befitted the occasion, 'Old Lilly' opened the bowling (the last time he would be seen in action) but, after sending down 44 deliveries at the expense of 22 runs, he complained of feeling unwell and had to leave the field. It was the one distressing note in an otherwise memorable and nostalgic game, which England won by 197 runs, Caesar striking 35 and 43 in confident fashion. Two arch-rivals must have enjoyed themselves, Wisden getting the wicket of Clarke, who later returned the compliment by bowling the little Sussex man.

From Caesar's viewpoint, Chaucer himself could not have composed a more delightful Canterbury Tale in mid-August when the sky glowed above a summer scene of cricket, flags, flowers and pretty dresses. Julius, once more playing for England, held the colourful stage and completed his maiden century. As he drove, cut and pulled his way through the seventies and eighties, excitement mounted. Although by now Caesar was able to 'jump in and drive the ball where he pleased', there were doubtless some nervous moments in the nineties before loud cheering greeted the finishing touch of his triumph.

Caesar's 101 included a five (off Edgar Willsher), nine fours and five threes, the innings ending when George Bennett caught him at long-stop off a ball from William Pilch, nephew of the famous Fuller. The warm acclamation that echoed from all corners of the ground as Julius walked from the middle would be forever fused in his memory. With Caffyn, Wisden, Dean and Sam Parr also making valuable contributions, England ran up a total of 324 and twice sliced through Kent to win by an innings and 179 runs.

One of several new laws introduced by MCC in 1854 concerned the use of runners for injured batsmen. As it happened, the first publicised dispute over its interpretation occurred at Lord's itself – during another encounter between England and Nottinghamshire – and, quite remarkably, Caesar again featured in a controversial incident. During his second innings, while batting with Wisden, he said he felt unfit (possibly gout, from which he increasingly suffered) and, having satisfied themselves on that point, the Notts men agreed to his having a runner. This turned out to be the Cambridge-born bowler, William Buttress, a lamplighter by trade and apparently given to eccentric behaviour.

Caesar was then run out – 'somewhat curiously', according to *Bell's Life.*

He drove a ball from Clarke and, forgetting the situation (and, presumably, his complaint), set off for a single; Buttress did not stir and was joined by Wisden at the striker's end. Caesar meanwhile made his ground at the bowler's end, but Clarke put down the wicket and appealed. The umpire, Tom Sewell, ruled that Caesar was not out, contending that Wisden should depart because the acting runner (Buttress) had not passed him and it therefore amounted to the same thing as both batsmen being at one end. Clarke and his colleagues then disputed the decision, refused to continue and left the field.

Bell's Life reported: 'After a long argument at the pavilion, it was decided that Caesar should go out. Neither the striker nor the substitute being off their ground, we are of the opinion (according to the law) that Wisden ought to have been given out, although the case would have been very hard indeed.'

Anyway, Nottinghamshire, for whom George Parr of the crouching stance scored 39 and 55, lost by 39 runs. Billy Buttress, despite a tendency to over-tipple, was a fine bowler of medium pace and played a prominent part in that defeat by taking nine wickets for three runs apiece. Fred Miller said that Buttress 'could almost make the ball speak' and once promised him £5 if United beat All-England, but, he added, 'I had to commit him to the care of Caffyn to ensure his remaining quite sober enough to bowl in the match.'

Surrey did not play at The Oval in 1854 because of their wrangle with the proprietor and, moreover, could arrange but a handful of away fixtures. (For a time, Caesar was installed by a member of the Marshall family in the newly-built Cricketers pub in Nightingale Road, Farncombe, where the serving of ale ensured no overall loss of income for the young batsman.) In anticipation of getting control of The Oval the following season, Surrey engaged a few new professionals. Among them was a tall 21-year-old called Stephenson with the distinguished forenames of Heathfield Harman. He soon established himself as a fine batsman, a fastish bowler able to whip the ball back disconcertingly from the off and, when needed, a very competent wicketkeeper. One contemporary doubted 'whether a finer all-round player ever went into the field'.

The All-England XI, which Stephenson would join later that season, were at Bristol in June playing Twenty-Two of the West Gloucester Club, and Caesar batted well in helping his side to a 149-run win. In a pony trap at the edge of the ground sat a little lad, not yet six, watching his father, who captained the local team. That bright-eyed boy, christened William Gilbert, was destined to bring a whole new dimension to cricket. His father's name was Dr Henry Mills Grace.

A 'brilliant display of cricket', wrote one journalist describing the three-day drawn game between Sussex and Surrey which began at Brighton on June 29 and produced no fewer than 636 runs. Caesar unleashed a fusillade of sparkling shots to make 77 before chasing a wide delivery and getting caught at cover-point by John Lillywhite. He was 'loudly and justly applauded' for his exhibition and followed it in the second innings with an aggressive 43.

Caesar must have felt confident that such form would clinch for him a place in the Players' side to meet The Gentlemen at Lord's in July. The fact that he did not appear had nothing to do with his batting, however. Along with Clarke, Caffyn and Parr, he was selected as expected, but the quartet 'would not play' because of a difference that had arisen between Clarke and MCC. With the quarrel still unresolved, the four again declined to turn out for England *against* MCC and, although probably influenced by Clarke, it must have been a frustrating time for Caesar, keen to consolidate his position in top-class cricket. A few weeks later, the dissenting foursome did take part in the England v Sussex match, but it might be regarded as significant that both Clarke and Parr 'guested' for the county, who won by 68 runs.

The return match that season between Surrey and Nottinghamshire was fought out at the Broadwater ground where, boosted by vocal support from fellow Godhelmians, Caesar made the best individual scores of 41 and 49 off the strong attack of Clarke, Bickley, Cris Tinley and Grundy. To his probable surprise and the overt delight of the partisan crowd, Julius even had a rare spell with the ball and succeeded in clean bowling Grundy and Clarke at the cost of a solitary run in three overs, and Surrey ran out winners by 65 runs. Caesar headed the county batting averages in 1854 with 35.28, a feat somewhat devalued by the paucity of fixtures.

Caesar's scores may not now seem very big, but they compared favourably with the best at that period. An individual century was then a rarity, and he scored three. Billy Caffyn, for example, managed two in his career and the great George Parr apparently only one in major matches. That is in no way to disparage those renowned batsmen, for both were acknowledged to have been more accomplished than was Caesar. It does indicate, however, that he was in the highest bracket at a time when runs were at a premium. That dearth has been linked to roughly the reign of roundarm bowling, the direction of which was difficult to control consistently and thus presented the batsmen with fewer opportunities. Increasingly higher scores were evident from 1858, when overarm, though still illegal until 1864, was being practised more and more.

While the popular touring sides galloped towards the end of the 1854 season, there passed from this world a cricketing monarch of whom it was said he would 'be remembered as long as the national game of England'. After a match in which the AEE were engaged at Primrose Hill, London, William Lillywhite, who was a spectator, could not resist a spot of bowling practice and he 'took' the wickets of some star batsmen. Now aged 62, this proved to be his final visit to a cricket ground. Within a fortnight, 'Old Lilly' was dead.

The AEE and UAEE seemed almost to dominate the cricket scene and pursued independent campaigns like opposing armies which never met. In the Crimea meanwhile, armed forces were battling for real with soldiers as bloody substitutes for wickets.

Far removed from such horrors, Julius Caesar spent part of the springtime of 1855 in the serenity of college life at Oxford – as a cricket coach. Other professionals similarly teaching the undergraduates amid the dreaming spires included Caffyn, Fuller Pilch, Hillyer, Hinkly and Grundy. In a match at the Magdalen ground in May, the young varsity men beat 'Eleven Professional Players Selected from the Twenty-Five Engaged by the University Clubs for the Season'. A clear case of the pupils outwitting their mentors, or was the 'defeat' perhaps a studied ploy by the professionals to underline their own worth as tutors? A pretty game, Mr Lillywhite might have remarked, but it ain't cricket.

Having overcome recent setbacks, Surrey CCC could now effectively direct operations at The Oval, and one of the first matches to be played there after a season's dormancy was that between the county and England. As William Clarke had some hand in the arrangements, the professionals loyal to the United All-England XI refused to take part. That Surrey (Caesar 24 and 18) lost by one wicket was due largely to another half-century by George Parr and also to some fine bowling by Bickley, whose deliveries came 'with a terrible pace from the pitch'.

To have seen Parr in full flow must have guaranteed an unforgettable experience, and an elm tree at Trent Bridge was named after him, so often did his favourite shot over midwicket chip its bark or send down a shower of leaves. Like Clarke, by whom he was introduced into top cricket, Parr could be testy and difficult, but he also had a very dry sense of humour. With apt solemnity, he would advise young cricketers to chat up the umpire: 'First of all enquire after his health, then say what a fine player his father was and, finally, present him with a brace of birds or rabbits. This will give you confidence and you will probably do well.'

That summer, Julius Caesar and H.H.Stephenson became embroiled in a dispute with the Surrey club. Both men were touring Lancashire with the All-England XI and refused, on grounds of expense, to appear for their county at Brighton. Authority at The Oval reacted in the strongest manner by deciding to do without them for the remainder of the season.

Although Surrey had concluded that the pair 'preferred Clarke to their county', *Bell's Life* told its readers, 'the players themselves gave as a reason that in playing for Clarke they had but to travel from Manchester, while no extra expenses were offered them to come from Manchester to Brighton, and that was the sole cause for their non-attendance. We mention this to show that no blame is to be attached to Clarke in using undue influence to keep them away, as we are sorry to hear was currently reported.'

So the estranged players continued to tour with the AEE, and Caesar, whose breezy form seemed unaffected by the suspension, showed up well. At Melton Mowbray he hit 70 before being bowled by a 'very easy ball' from Frank Tinley. Then, against Twenty-Two of West Gloucestershire at Bristol, he reeled off 33 and 78, batting in his second innings as 'every lover of cricket delights to see', and had reached 60 before giving a chance. Another feature of the game, which the AEE won by 167 runs, was the appearance in the home side of Dr Grace and three of his sons, Henry (aged 22), Alfred (15) and Edward Mills (13). The exciting impact of that family on the world of cricket lay not far around the corner.

Caesar and Stephenson were reinstated by Surrey the next season, which also marked the end of an era. Even the shrewd William Clarke could not outwit the Grim Reaper but, with typical stubbornness, he took a wicket with the very last ball he bowled – for the AEE at Whitehaven on June 16, 1856. Only then, weak from illness, did he dodder from the field. He died at his London home in Wandsworth Road on August 25, aged 57.

During his cricket career, which spanned four decades, Clarke had helped immensely to heighten the appeal and standard of the game by taking his pioneering All-England XI to the people. Julius Caesar had good reason overall to be grateful to the man.

Chapter Seven

Clash of the Giants

It seemed a natural progression that George Parr would take over the leadership of the All-England XI. He had been close to Clarke, was a competent organiser, respected by his colleagues, among the very best batsmen in the land, and his association with the AEE went back to August 1847 when, going in at number nine against Twenty-Two of Leicestershire, he made exactly 100. His formal appointment as secretary and confirmation as captain took place on September 26, 1856 and was accompanied by a dash of democracy in the election of a management committee consisting of Caesar, Willsher, Anderson, H.H.Stephenson and Alfred Clarke. No longer would it be a one-man band.

Among the AEE newcomers was John Jackson, of Nottinghamshire, then aged 23 and reputedly the fastest bowler yet seen. He certainly measured up to the part, topping six-feet and amply filling an oak-strong frame. On dismissing a batsman, Jackson was said almost invariably to pull out a handkerchief into which he resoundingly blew his nose and, because of this peculiarity, became known as 'Foghorn'. He possessed a wry wit and once confessed that while he had never taken all 10 wickets in an innings, he managed something equally satisfying by getting nine for The North against The South and, in the process, laming John Wisden so that he could not continue.

Ironically, a leg injury cut short Jackson's career and he did not play much after 1866. His popularity and service were acknowledged at a benefit match in Nottingham in 1874 to the extent of £265, but he later found difficulty in making ends meet and from being 'the best bowler in the world' drifted into obscurity. 'Foghorn' died in a workhouse in 1901.

The 1856 season proved moderately successful for Julius Caesar, whose best performance was as highest scorer in his debut in the traditional Gentlemen v Players match at Lord's in July. He made 51 in his 'usual quick and brilliant hitting style', his side winning by two wickets. It was no easy matter to get runs at Lord's, where the pitch, although improving, remained notorious. One bruised professional remarked that the only resemblance between it and a billiards table were the pockets. No less an authority than

Caffyn left a vivid picture: 'Oh, those shooters at Lord's. One or two balls as high as your head; then, perhaps, one in the ribs and, then, a shooter. No wonder when we stopped one of these, we were greeted with a round of applause.'

Nevertheless, Lord's continued to stage the majority of important matches and it was the venue for the long and eagerly awaited first-ever clash between the All-England XI and the United All-England XI. With Clarke gone, earlier objections to such an intriguing encounter vanished and the event, in aid of the recently-revived Cricketers' Fund Friendly Society (of which Caesar was a committee member), marked the start of what would become the most prestigious fixture in the cricket calendar for the next few years. That three-day inaugural game began on June 1, 1857, when around 10,000 spectators, including many noblemen and well-known patrons of the sport, assembled in warm sunshine. Even the pitch appeared to be more presentable than usual and, in the view of *Bell's Life*, 'played pretty well'.

Wisden won the toss and sent in Thomas Hunt and Dean to face the lively AEE attack of Jackson and Willsher. The United totalled 143, due in no small measure to Caffyn, who displayed 'some good cricket' to get 38, and Dean, who made 36. Jackson, still a relatively new menace, bowled very straight and his fierce pace on the hard surface 'told tales' to the extent that he finished with 6 for 31. All-England, for whom Parr scored 56 not out, replied with 106. An ankle injury to Wisden, who was unable to bowl much, handicapped United, but the versatile Caffyn stepped up to take seven wickets for 69, among them that of Caesar, whom he got out for 9. United's second innings of 140 left the AEE to get 78, a mission accomplished for the loss of five wickets.

That first battle, though absorbing, perhaps failed to live up to its very high expectations and pre-match hype. One commentator thought he knew why. 'It cannot for one moment be doubted,' he wrote, 'that had the veteran Clarke brought the team into the field, the interest would have been far greater.'

The teams met for the return at Lord's at the end of July, the AEE being successful again, this time by 133 runs, in a benefit match for James Dean, who reportedly cleared upwards of £350. A dressing-room disagreement delayed the start because of the AEE's intention to replace the injured Anderson with another Yorkshireman, Teddy Stephenson. United objected strongly to this last-minute proposal, pointing out that Stephenson was not a regular member of the AEE who, in any case, should have brought along a *bona fide* substitute knowing, as they did, that Anderson was unlikely to be fit.

United eventually took the field, but the arguments did not abate until after a number of wickets had fallen. Only then was it mutually agreed that Thomas Hunt, United's 12th man and formerly an AEE player, could turn out for the latter. When they embarked upon their second innings, United needed 188 for victory, but the bowling of Willsher and Jackson was of 'too terrific a nature to allow more than 54 runs to be obtained' and the batsmen 'appeared to completely give themselves up to it; they went out like shelling peas'.

Surrey enjoyed another outstanding season in 1858. In fact, they had not lost a county match for three years, much of their success emanating from F.P.Miller, who instilled a sense of purpose and pride into his team. Currently described as being a 'synonym for the finest cricket of the day', Surrey had won all five of their first-class fixtures in 1856, all nine the following year and in 1858 (Frederick Burbidge's first of eight seasons as captain) gained five wins and a draw in a six-match programme.

Among Caesar's newer county colleagues was George ('Ben') Griffith, whose hurricane hitting found more favour with the crowds than with bowlers. Other counties, too, were producing fresh, exciting stars, not least Cambridgeshire, whose rapid rise in the cricket firmament owed much to the batting of Thomas Hayward and Robert Carpenter. A willowy figure of 'gloomy' countenance, Hayward personified frailty at the crease. By comparison, Carpenter reflected the rudeness of health and his drives were likened to a 'horse kicking'.

Joining the ranks of the All-England XI that year was Nottinghamshire's Richard Daft, then 22 and a classic batsman later to be spoken of in the same breath as the incomparable Grace. Hayward also swelled the AEE ranks, while Carpenter threw in his substantial lot with United. When the teams met at Lord's in July the AEE, triumphant by an innings and 79 runs, did George Parr proud. Or did they? The scheduled three-day match for his benefit ended in two.

Julius Caesar played in a warm-hearted affair that August organised financially to assist William Hillyer, the popular Kent bowler, whose career ended abruptly three years earlier when he injured a hand and whose health had now begun a tragic tubercular decline. The Surrey club committee granted the use of The Oval for this special game and, moreover, there was a splendid response from the country's most famous players invited to appear. A strong England XI played Eighteen Veterans whose line-up read like a cricketers' role of honour, past champions rallying to raise money for one of their friends. Kent's Ted Wenman, at 54, was the oldest, and others included Alfred Mynn (aged 51), Dean (42), Brockwell (46), Box (49), Henry Sampson (45) of Yorkshire, Thomas Adams (45) of Kent, and from Surrey, John Heath (50) and Tom Sewell (52). The fact that England won easily by nine wickets meant little. What mattered was that Hillyer, who had less than three years to live, received about £400 to help make his final months a little more comfortable.

When Julius Caesar returned home at the end of the season to winter in Godalming, he had no inkling that in a year's time he would be some 3000 miles away on a unique cricket tour. He and his family now lived in a terraced house in Ockford Road, close to the Richmond Arms and not far from the pepper-pot town hall. Their home, comprising four principal rooms (two up and two down), a wash-place and a cellar, was then owned by Mrs Sarah Marshall, of Broadwater House, to whom Caesar paid annual rent of 12 guineas. The house has long since been demolished and the site built over.

The 1861 census shows that living next door at that time was Mark Major, a baker/grocer, and his family, and, residing at that same address, a 22-year-old baker/journeyman, James Street – almost certainly the Cranleigh-born pace bowler, who would play for Surrey (1863-78) and umpire a Test match between England and Australia at The Oval in 1890.

A daughter, Ann Jane, had been born to the Caesars on February 7, 1857, but, sadly, by that autumn of 1858 she was already three-quarters of the way through her brief life. The little girl's death would be the first of a number of unhappy and harrowing experiences to be suffered by Julius Caesar in the forthcoming years.

Chapter Eight

Transatlantic Adventure

S hortly before the trees shed flurries of autumnal russet and gold, the first England cricket team to tour overseas left Liverpool in September 1859 for Canada and the United States.

Chiefly responsible for making the arrangements were W.P.Pickering, the former Cambridge University player prominently associated with the Montreal Cricket Club, Edmond Wilder, of Sussex CCC and president of the Cricketers' Fund Friendly Society, and the enterprising Fred Lillywhite. George Parr and Johnny Wisden, as secretaries respectively of the All-England XI and the United All-England XI, also figured in the negotiations, which provided for each player to receive a basic £50 and an all-expenses-paid trip.

The team – six members apiece from the AEE and UAEE – comprised George Parr (aged 33) captain, James Grundy (35) and John Jackson (26) of Nottinghamshire; Julius Caesar (29), William Caffyn (31), Thomas Lockyer (32) and H.H.Stephenson (26) of Surrey; John Lillywhite (32) and John Wisden (33) of Sussex; Robert Carpenter (28), Alfred ('Ducky') Diver (35) and Thomas Hayward (24) of Cambridgeshire. Fred Lillywhite (30) accompanied the party as official chronicler, carting with him his printing press and tent.

The past summer had revealed most of those selected to be in grand form. Hayward, for instance, played a fine innings of 220 at Fenner's early that season, Caffyn (157) and Parr (130) recorded career-best scores, Jemmy Grundy also hit a century and, in a blistering spell of bowling, Jackson had plundered 10 wickets for a single run.

Caesar had not played in the latter part of May and not much in June either, reportedly because of injury – a bout of gout, perhaps – but an additional reason could have been the illness and resultant death from whooping-cough on May 25 of his two-year-old daughter. As Jane Caesar was expecting another child in August, it would be nice to think of her husband extending his absence from cricket to be of homely comfort at that distressing time.

When a saddened Caesar returned to the game, touring the West Country

51

with the AEE, he witnessed a phenomenal piece of bowling. The sight of 'Foghorn' Jackson advancing to unleash a thunderbolt was enough to disturb the vitals of any batsman, and it cannot be claimed that the Twenty-Two of Cornwall looked much above third-rate. Nevertheless, the performance of Jackson at Redruth in removing 10 of them in 49 deliveries for the outlay of a solitary run amounted to sheer roundarmed robbery and one wonders just how those nose membranes stood up to the strain. Cornwall were routed for 22. After the AEE had totalled 226, of which Parr sculpted a near-flawless 101, the Cornishmen replied with a paltry 30 for 16 wickets before conceding defeat.

Parr's highest-ever score of 130 had been for Nottinghamshire at The Oval in mid-July when they beat Surrey by eight wickets. After his innings, Parr was greeted by William Burrup, the Surrey secretary, who told him: 'In this match, you have made one of the finest displays of batting even seen on this or any other ground. On this ground, we do not ask where a player comes from, but at once reward him for exhibiting fine play.' Burrup then handed Parr £2 from the club and an extra £13 collected from spectators. Future events would see the two men on far less friendly terms.

Surrey, who had carried all before them in the three previous seasons, were unaccustomed to losing. That defeat by arch-rivals Nottinghamshire tasted bitter, but they descended with an even bigger bump soon afterwards when England drubbed them by 392 runs. Only rarely in one match had one player held such sway as did that gifted amateur, V.E.Walker, then 22 years of age. Bowling superbly, he took all the county's first-innings wickets for 74 and then followed up by scoring 108 in England's second innings. On their return to the crease, the Surrey batsmen were massacred for 39, those pleading guilty to justifiable homicide being Jackson (6 for 21) and Walker (4 for 17). Caesar had the dubious distinction of being the only one to escape Walker's clutches, making 16 not out and 3. (Those successive defeats were the only two sustained in 1859 by Surrey, who won their other seven matches.)

Caesar was at Manchester in August when some ill-tempered heat was generated after an incident in the North v Surrey game. Teddy Stephenson, the northerners' wicketkeeper, hurt his hand during the visitors' first innings of 189 and the following day, when The North had lost six wickets, F.P.Miller (acting-skipper for the county) rejected a request for a substitute to bat. After several sharp exchanges, Stephenson started to walk to the middle

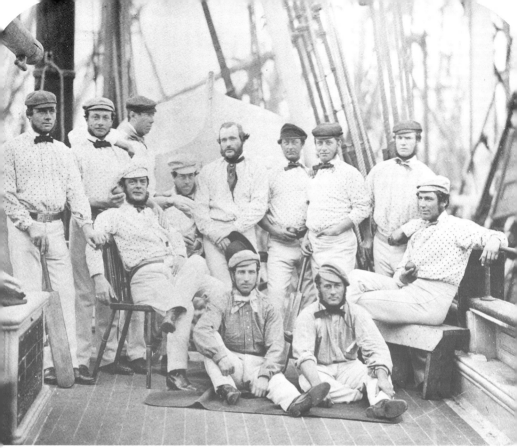

England's Twelve Champion Cricketers, ready for the voyage to North America in 1859, the first major international cricket tour: Robert Carpenter, Billy Caffyn, Tom Lockyer, John Wisden (seated), H. H. Stephenson, George Parr (captain), Jem Grundy, Julius Caesar, Tom Hayward, John Jackson; in front: Alfred Diver, John Lillywhite.

intending to bat one-handed. The cheers of the crowd turned to a hubbub of dissension when Parr emerged from the sidelines and promptly ordered Stephenson to return. This he did and Surrey went on to win what must have been an unpleasant contest. The matter undoubtedly rankled Parr, who would later indicate his dislike of southern clubs and of Surrey in particular.

On September 2, shortly before leaving Godalming to join other players in the England side for the transatlantic tour, Julius Caesar informed the district registrar of an addition to the family – a son, Julius, born on August 7, and who, when he grew up, would cause his father much heartache.

There was, too, a gathering of 'friends and lovers of cricket' at the King's Arms Hotel to 'pay a complimentary farewell' to Caesar, who promised to do all he could to 'uphold the fame of England and her national game'. The *Surrey Standard* added that 'the proceedings, which were diverted of all formalities, assumed a purely harmonious character and song and sentiment were passed round with a hearty zest'.

While Caesar travelled to Liverpool to embark upon the then longest journey of his life, hundreds of his fellow townsfolk were off on what for many of them was also their farthest trip from home. They converged on the brand new Godalming station for the first cheap-day rail excursion on the recently-completed direct line to Portsmouth. Certainly the cricketers would have wished for an equally smooth crossing to Canada in the *Nova Scotian*, which sailed from Merseyside on September 7. The rolling Atlantic was at its most disagreeable. The vessel pitched and groaned and most passengers turned a fashionable shade of pallid green as high creamy seas sorted out the landlubbers from the sailors.

A gale blew the ship miles off course and she eventually arrived at Quebec well behind schedule. The latter stages of the storm-enforced detour had taken her past huge icebergs that, for all their glinting grandeur, hardly reminded the party of cricket. However, spirits revived on reaching the broad St Lawrence with its spectacular scenery and, as Julius Caesar commented in a dispatch to the *West Surrey Times*, 'the unpleasantness of the voyage was soon forgotten in the delightful prospect afforded on either side'. Soon after disembarking at Quebec, the players were whisked on to a train for Montreal and the start of a five-match programme against teams of 22 as well as several supplementary matches.

Arriving at the hotel, the Englishmen received an enthusiastic welcome from the waiting crowd – the first of many during the tour. The opening fixture had been advertised to take place on September 21 (the tourists were still aboard ship) and many people turned up only to be disappointed. The match got under way three days later, however, before an attendance of about 3000 at the compact Montreal ground 'prettily situated at the foot of an immense mountain'. Heavy rain had deadened the pitch, and Caffyn and Jackson, who launched the attack against Twenty-Two of Canada (mainly expatriate Britons), could get little pace. Even so, the bowling proved more than enough for most batsmen and Canada were all out for 85, Jackson taking seven wickets, Caffyn five and Parr, with his 'slows', mopping up the

Touring 1859 style: the English cricketers bravely endeavour to dine during an Atlantic gale: sketch from Fred Lillywhite's book.

tail to get six for eight runs. The visitors (only Caesar failed to score) went on to win by eight wickets.

A series of banquets, with diplomatic speeches, punctuated the tour, and the Englishmen enjoyed lavish hospitality. During the first such function F.G.Johnson, the Montreal club's president, extolled the virtues of cricket, the home country and the British Empire and, almost predictably, referred to the presence in the company of 'one with a classic name'. He hoped, however, that Caesar would not emulate his namesake Roman emperor by saying *Veni, Vidi, Vici* (cheers and laughter). Parr, who replied, could not also fail to draw applause when he declared: 'We are very much surprised at the cricket we have met here. We have gone to many parts of England and not met such cricket.' Only a cynic might have detected some unwitting ambiguity in that.

Pictures of the tourists appeared in magazines and, according to the *Toronto Globe*, one lady confided to Caesar, sitting next to her on a crowded train, what a 'horrid, plain-looking set of men' they were. Julius, who prided himself on his personal appearance, replied politely that he was one of them. The poor woman sank into an embarrassed silence but, before she alighted, found the courage and grace to concede that if they all looked like him then they were 'not such a bad-looking set of fellows after all'. Conscious of their role as sporting ambassadors, the party set out to be complimentary and courteous and, after crossing the 49th Parallel into the United States, again experienced very friendly receptions. The tourists were sumptuously entertained and sightseeing trips took in the thundering Niagara Falls over which a little earlier that year Blondin, the famous French acrobat, had walked on a tightrope.

The cricketers made front-page news in the *New York Times* for some days, while other newspapers also gave considerable column inches to the international match with Twenty-Two of the United States. The event was staged by the St George's Club of New York on their ground located a short ferry ride away at Hoboken, New Jersey. Thousands flocked to see the England XI in action, play starting on October 4 with a 'cool breeze agreeably tempering the sun's rays'. It soon became apparent that a vast gulf separated the teams and the home side were toppled in two hours for 38. Carpenter and Hayward, who walked to the wicket to the stirring strains of *Rule Britannia*, then put on 60 in 90 minutes before the former was caught and the visitors continued unobstructed, eventually to win by an innings and 64 runs.

According to one newspaper, the United States 'never had a chance; they have a lot of middling players who live by cricket, but they are mere children in the hands of these English players'. On their return to New York the 'excitement was intense', each player being called in turn by numerous admirers and prompting fresh cheering. An animated crowd followed the team through the streets and applauded them to the entrance of the Astor House Hotel.

After that lopsided game at Hoboken, the *New York Herald* confidently predicted that the Twenty-Two of Philadelphia would give a much better account of themselves 'especially as the majority of the players are Americans'. In front of another big crowd, the Philadelphians did indeed put up a stronger resistance, although they lost a low-scoring match by seven wickets. The same newspaper was quick to conclude that because the side was 'composed principally of Americans' it had been able to outshine the Canadian and New York teams, whose players are 'nearly all Englishmen'.

Like his colleagues, Caesar strove to be a well-mannered and tactful guest, but he failed on at least one occasion and almost suffered a severe, if not fatal, consequence. Having found a bar selling London porter, he downed too many pints, became embroiled in an argument with a New Yorker and threatened to knock his block off. Explaining that he did not descend to brawling, the piqued American announced 'here is my card' and brandished a revolver. A shaken Caesar somehow sweet-talked his way towards a hasty retreat and raced back to the hotel. In the safety of the morning after, Julius was said to have told his team-mates that 'the first Yankee I meet on British ground I'll give a hiding to – even if I get three months for it'.

Caesar was usually to the fore with off-the-field skylarking. Stephenson and he often acted the fool in the Surrey dressing-room and probably performed the same comedy duo on tour as well. The former could put his thumb out of joint and had the habit of creeping up behind Caesar and clicking it in his ear. Julius hated it, or at least pretended to, and would hurl something at his retreating companion. Then the pair might go into a song-and-dance routine with Julius hopping about in time to Stephenson's whistling; as the tempo quickened, so would the party-piece, which usually ended with both men gasping for breath and collapsing with laughter.

One person Caesar never riled with his teasing was the equable Johnny Wisden. The little Sussex man once started to grow a moustache, a tempting target for a jibe. 'I've never seen such a guy in all my life,' taunted Caesar. 'What on earth do you let that thing grow for?' An unruffled Wisden responded affably: 'Oh, to make myself look uglier, if it's possible.'

By contrast, Fred Lillywhite seems to have been less easy-going. He fussed unduly about his printing press and scoring tent which, according to him, Parr objected to his bringing out of England at all although it was 'entirely upon my own risk and speculation, so that the Press in that country, as well as in this, should not be misinformed'. Lillywhite never forgot Parr's alleged attempt to 'do me a serious injury'. Once, the valuable equipment was inadvertently left behind at Buffalo and no scorecards were available for the first day (October 17) of the match with Twenty-Two of Upper Canada at Hamilton where, despite that oversight and the biting cold, the tourists won by 10 wickets.

Wretched weather continued for the final game – at Rochester – against Twenty-Two of the United States and Canada which began on October 21 and was interrupted by snow! It ended in victory by an innings and 68 runs for England, whose players took the field on the last day wrapped in mufflers, gloves and overcoats. Notwithstanding the arctic conditions,

Wisden took no fewer than 29 wickets including six in successive deliveries. So the England XI, declining several offers to meet the Americans at baseball, completed an all-victorious campaign. The crossing home, this time aboard *North Briton*, was again rough and, much to the relief of passengers, the ship reached Liverpool in one piece on November 11. The tour had been highly successful and, according to Caffyn, each player made about £90 as well as gifts showered upon them by generous hosts.

Less than a month later, the southern members of that team were guests of honour at a celebration dinner at the King's Arms Hotel in Caesar's home town. Henry Marshall (Surrey president) was in the chair and, besides the tourists – Caesar, Caffyn, Stephenson, Lockyer and John Lillywhite (Wisden absent owing to illness) – the large company included other Surrey and Sussex professionals plus the brothers John and V.E. Walker, the twins William and John Burrup, Fred Lillywhite, Godalming civic dignitaries and members of local cricket clubs.

The Union Jack and Stars and Stripes hung above the top table and the whole room was festooned with emblems, evergreens, flowers and large pictures of the touring side. At five o'clock, the gathering sat down to tackle a 'most excellent repast' and after liberal dining and wining came a lengthy list of toasts. These ranged from 'The Queen and Prince Albert' and 'The Army and Navy' by way of 'The Surrey Club' and 'The Mayor and Corporation' to 'The Press' and 'Fred Lillywhite' and not forgetting, of course, 'The Scorers and Umpires'.

In replying to 'The Twelve Cricketers', Julius Caesar made a real *faux pas*. The party had been very well received in Canada, he declared, but he 'could not say as much for the United States'. Whether that injudicious remark was prompted by some personal grievance (even, perhaps, a semi-humorous allusion to his bar-room clash with the gun-toting American), a glass too many of wine, a Freudian slip or a pure misunderstanding, newspapers in the States took most unkindly to his unfavourable comment and said so. Fred Lillywhite was also far from happy about it and regretted that 'such words should have dropped from so renowned a cricketer'. It does appear inexplicable.

In common with most batsmen in the rain-affected season of 1860, Caesar derived little return and, to some extent, his fear of being dropped became a reality. He was omitted from the national team on two occasions and, at Lord's in July, found himself in the 'Next Fourteen' against 'Eleven

How the cream of English cricket came close to ending up under the depths of the Atlantic on the way home. SS North Briton *is tossed violently, and loses her jib-boom.*

against The Gentlemen, twice for The South v The North and also played for the All-England XI, whose latest recruit was George Tarrant, of Cambridgeshire.

'Tear-'Em' Tarrant, then 21, generated a scorching pace during the brief time he fretted and strutted upon cricket's stage and could be ferocious for short spells before blowing himself out. Sadly, the young man tended to lose his cool if things went against him, and it seems that success, as well as addiction to ale, went to his head. (Shortly after his early death in 1870, a poem by 'Batsman' asserted that Tarrant wore 'the wreath of honour in a random way'.)

For all that, Tarrant's searing speed made more of an impact on the 1860 season than did Caesar's batting. With top scores of 45 not out for Surrey (v Sussex) in June and 43 for The Players a month later, Julius totalled only 254 in 24 innings. But he would soon bounce back.

Chapter Nine

Sunshine and Shadow

Warm weather and some big scores marked the summer of 1861, but it was not only the sun that raised the temperature and cast sharp shadows over the cricket scene. Before the season was out, ill-feeling arose among professional players about the first-ever England team to tour Australia – the start of an unpleasant rift that would remain for much of the decade.

That apart, it was a rewarding time for Julius Caesar, whose 'punishing, lively, hearty and brilliant hitting' brought him the second century of his career. Attacks of gout caused him considerable discomfort, sometimes acutely enough to prevent his playing at all, but on his day he was as exciting as any batsman in the land and always popular with spectators.

Probably the season's outstanding match was played at The Oval during the last week in June when Surrey and Cambridgeshire rattled up no fewer than 976 runs between them before victory went to the latter by two wickets. There had not been three centuries in one match since 1817 (when Lambert, getting two, and 'Squire' Osbaldeston did so at Lord's), but now came a hundred apiece from three different players – Caesar, Hayward and Carpenter.

Surrey reached 228 in their first innings, of which Caesar had a bright knock of exactly 50, which earned him prolonged applause and a sovereign in talent money. The visitors lost two wickets for 10 before Hayward joined Carpenter to add 125 by the close of the first day. The pair continued in sprightly form the next morning and not until the total stood at 222 were they separated, Carpenter being caught by Mortlock for precisely 100. Hayward went a little later to a catch by Caffyn, again off the bowling of Tom Sewell (junior), and with Fred Bell getting 50 not out, Cambridgeshire had established a strong lead of 101.

By the end of the second day, Surrey had fallen to 141 for 7 in reply. Caesar had gone in with the new 'telegraph' box showing a dismal 30 for 3 and, at stumps, was 64 not out, the 'brilliant display of cricket' resulting in his being called by members to the pavilion, where 'many very handsome presents were made to him'.

A large crowd assembled at The Oval on the final day – a Saturday – when, for nearly two hours, Caesar dominated the crease. He completed his century to the accompaniment of loud cheering and went on to 111 before falling to a slip catch by Hayward off 'Tear'Em' Tarrant, being ninth out with the score on 249. His fine innings, for which he collected another 'talent sovereign', included a five and seven fours.

Cambridgeshire got the 159 needed for victory with two wickets to spare, despite some steady bowling by Sewell (5 for 55 in 34 overs). The Surrey club and spectators subscribed the sum of £48-10s which was shared by Caesar (£22), Carpenter and Hayward (£9 each) and Sewell (£8-10s). Bell, who had made a half-century and taken nine wickets in the match, had to be content with only a sovereign – a 'hard measure' not overlooked by one indignant reader of aptly-named *Bell's Life*, who wrote a letter of protest to the editor.

Caesar and H.H.Stephenson missed out on the South v North game at Lord's because they 'were not asked in time', whatever dilatory liaison that implied, but they appeared for Surrey against The North just afterwards. A confident Caesar took 21 and 29 off a strong attack led by Jackson, Tarrant and Tinley. The honours and sympathy, however, went to Caffyn, who finished only two short of his century in the second innings. In a match producing 832 runs, Surrey gained victory by 92 over the visitors, for whom Carpenter, Daft and Hayward each hit more than 60 in their first innings.

An aggregate of 870 runs was recorded at The Oval in July when Surrey, with six injured players, beat England by 56 in what became dubbed the 'Cripple Match'. Caffyn was lame, Sewell dislocated a thumb, Mortlock's thumb was also damaged, William Mudie was badly hurt by a ball from Jackson, skipper Burbidge split a hand and, to add to Surrey's problems, Stephenson was suffering from acute diarrhoea. England's V.E.Walker had a dicky knee.

The duels between the All-England XI and the United All-England XI continued to attract very big crowds. The third that season (AEE won the first at Lord's in June by six runs; the second, at Old Trafford in July, was drawn) took place at The Oval in early August, the UAEE winning by 115 runs. Caesar had the unusual experience of being bowled (for a duck) by county compatriot Caffyn, but came back with an arresting 72 in his second innings.

The 1861 season ended on a discordant note, the repercussions of which would rumble on for years. It started when overtures were being made for an England side to play in Australia (the first to go 'Down Under'), sponsored by Felix Spiers and Christopher Pond, partners in the Melbourne firm of caterers. Their agent, W.B.Mallam, arrived in Britain during August to undertake the arrangements. He duly contacted members of various county clubs and, on the 22nd, invited to dinner at the Griffin Hotel, Manchester, professionals then appearing in the North v Surrey match. The offer he put forward was a basic £150 per player plus expenses to cover travel and accommodation.

George Parr and others rejected the proposals but the Surrey secretary, William Burrup, was attributed with saying that, if terms were agreed, Caffyn, Sewell, H.H.Stephenson, Mortlock, Carpenter, Hayward, Tarrant, Daft, Jackson and E.Stephenson would be willing to go. Exactly how strong a brief he had to speak on behalf of the non-Surrey men is uncertain but, in the event, his optimistic forecast was to prove ill-founded. Players were given time to consider the matter further, although it seems that even at that stage some of those originally invited – among them Caesar, Parr, Lockyer, Willsher, Grundy and Anderson – had already made up their minds to stay at home. Insufficient money was given as the determining factor, but there was also probably a measure of pique at the way in which the initial negotiations had been handled.

It so happened that the next occasion on which the principal parties assembled was on Caesar's doorstep at the Broadwater ground, where Twenty-Two of Godalming, Guildford and District began a three-day match with the All-England XI on September 2. Henry Marshall, the Surrey president, Burrup and Mallam were there; so were eight of the professionals who had played at Manchester a fortnight earlier, plus Caesar, whose gouty foot had kept him out of several recent games. The proposed visit to Australia must surely have been a major topic of conversation among promoters and players alike and, whether or not the gathering was fortuitous, there would have been ample opportunity for further bargaining. If, indeed, any last-minute attempts were made to induce a change of heart, then Mallam and his supporters faced disappointment. In fact, even most of those whom Burrup had earlier indicated as ready to go if terms were acceptable spurned the offer and, significantly, the final twelve selected included no fewer than seven Surrey men.

At a meeting in Birmingham on September 6 during the North v South game, H.H.Stephenson was 'unanimously chosen' to captain the tourists, the others being: William Caffyn, William Mortlock, George Griffith, Tom Sewell, William Mudie and Charles Lawrence (all of Surrey); Tom Hearne (Middlesex); Teddy Stephenson and Roger Iddison (Yorkshire); George Bennett (Kent); George ('Tiny') Wells (Sussex). The team far from reflected England's best, of course. In truth, those refusing to go represented just about the most powerful eleven, give or take a couple of players, in the country at that time.

It is just possible that part of Julius Caesar's reason for not going on the trip concerned the fact that his wife was again pregnant. The son to whom she would give birth at their home in Ockford Road, Godalming, on January 23, 1862 was to be named Charles Benjamin.

Not a few people wondered just how big a role George Parr, as leader of the AEE, played in the decision of so many top cricketers not to tour. He was an influential man and, by all accounts, was upset by Burrup's part in the negotiations. It was further said that Parr and other northerners disapproved of Stephenson being captain which, on the face of it, smacks a bit like a dog-in-the-manger reaction particularly if they had resolved not to participate.

It was strongly held in some quarters that while Parr negotiated with Mallam, the Surrey secretary intervened, underbid and used his position to advance the interests of Stephenson as skipper. Whatever the rights and wrongs, it became clear that there was no love lost between Parr and his adherents on the one hand and Burrup and the Surrey club on the other.

Fred Lillywhite later wrote that it was he upon whom Mallam first called regarding the tour. 'I consequently introduced him to Mr Burrup and he was then introduced to Mr H.Marshall, the president, and several others, not only in the Surrey club, but members of the principal clubs in the North,' claimed Lillywhite. 'We managed to get a team together without George Parr and school; consequently his temper would not allow him to relish it, so that he has wrongly and unjustly fought the honorary secretary of the Surrey club instead of challenging me, as I held the belt for the time being.'

So, amid recriminations, Stephenson and his team sailed from England on October 20 aboard Brunel's *Great Britain* for a series of 12 games against numerically superior opponents. The outfitting firm of John Lillywhite fulfilled an order for apparel including caps, ties and belts (all of dark blue) and white flannel shirts. Each player also received a new pair of pads.

The Englishmen arrived in Melbourne on Christmas Eve and began their first match – with Eighteen of Victoria – on New Year's Day 1862 before a shirt-sleeved crowd estimated at 15,000. As the England XI took the field, a brass band struck up the National Anthem, the last strains of which were drowned by a 'tremendous burst of cheering'. The tourists, who were treated almost like royalty wherever they went, won six and drew four of the dozen official fixtures and, after the final match at Melbourne on March 20-24, they planted commemorative elm trees. Lawrence, who also played for Middlesex and New South Wales, remained in Australia to coach at a Sydney club. (He later coached the aboriginal team and brought them to England for a tour in 1868, which included a drawn match with Godalming CC at Broadwater, probably watched by Julius Caesar, who by then had retired from the game.)

Except for Lawrence and Wells, who slightly prolonged his stay, the trailblazing party arrived home on May 12. During their antipodean absence, cricket had lost two of its best-loved personalities. That gentle giant, Alfred Mynn, died at his brother's home in London on November 1, 1861. He was 54, had been a central figure for some 30 years and, in a memorial poem, W.J.Prowse ended poignantly: 'Lightly lie the turf upon thee, kind and manly Alfred Mynn'. Less than four months later another of cricket's leviathans, who had taken his last bow at Lord's 11 years before Mynn first played there, also departed this earth – 'Silver Billy' Beldham at the Methuselah-like age of 96.

Chapter Ten

The Day of the No-Ball

While the standing of the mid-Victorian professional cricketer had grown considerably during the previous two decades, it still behoved him to recognise his place in the pecking order and, outwardly at least, to acknowledge it. Some of them might aspire to a sort of superficial social parity with the game's administrators, patrons and amateur players but in reality the gulf of class remained as wide as ever.

Julius Caesar, who was certainly no sycophant, appreciated the situation nonetheless and once stated publicly that professionals ought to heed their conduct because 'if it were not for the pecuniary assistance of the gentlemen, cricket would soon cease to occupy the position it now holds'. Although he could be suspected of wishing to feather his own nest since he was speaking in the presence of the Marshall family, he was only expressing an obvious truth.

A professional in the 1860s could by no means rely solely on cricket for a living. There were comparatively few matches for many of them and the basic appearance money not very lucrative, although some of the top performers would derive additional revenue from benefit matches. After his playing career, he might devote more time to his original trade or, perhaps, secure a post as coach at a public school or become an innkeeper, trusting no doubt that his 'name' would attract extra custom. For some, however, the end of active cricket signalled the start of a slide which led to abject circumstances. Then the former hero of the hour was often shunned and, finally, forgotten.

Such melancholy thoughts were probably far from Caesar's mind in 1862. Of much greater concern was another cricket conflict, the outcome of which would legally permit the bowling arm to be raised above shoulder-level. An incident at The Oval on August 26 was to jolt the law-makers, anger players and test personal friendships. The match between Surrey and England had entered the twilight stages of the second day's play and the leading actors in the drama about to unfold were the Kent left-arm fast bowler Edgar Willsher and umpire John Lillywhite.

England had totalled a mammoth 503 (then the highest innings to date) over the best part of two days, of which Hayward made 117 and shared in a stand of 153 with Carpenter, who was out for 94. Grundy (95) and Willsher (54) had earlier shared in an opening partnership of 124, immediately after which Daft fell to a 'very bad ball' for 0. Surrey paid dearly for fielding lapses – Mortlock dropped Grundy, then Willsher was missed by Lockyer, making 'that worthy scratch his head' and, early in his innings, Hayward skyed the ball, which the 'slanting rays of the sun effectually prevented' Edward Dowson from catching.

Surrey began their reply as the clock struck six, Mortlock facing Willsher, who bowled from the pavilion end, and having an early shock when his partner, Tom Humphrey, a 23-year-old nicknamed 'Pocket Hercules', was out without scoring. Burbidge joined Mortlock.

Then, in Willsher's third over, it happened. John Lillywhite shouted 'No-ball!' The bowler may even have grinned just then, but any good humour rapidly gave way to disbelief and mounting indignation when he was 'called' a further five times in succession. Much uncertainty existed around the ground until, as a reporter for *The Sporting Life* later observed, 'it began to dawn on the imagination that at length an umpire had been found possessing sufficient moral courage to carry out Law No 10'. Indeed, many umpires had for years tended to ignore the ruling about the height of the bowling arm.

A disgusted Willsher slung the ball away and accompanied by all but two of the England team (the amateurs V.E.Walker and the Hon.C.G.Lyttelton) left the field. Many excited spectators surrounded John Lillywhite, who remained in the middle until the appointed time for drawing stumps at seven o'clock. Cheers and counter-cheers rent the confused air and it was said Caesar 'got so wrath with the crowd that his pugilistic tendencies were in danger of being called into play'.

Inside the pavilion, altercations broke out. Henry Marshall hastily summoned a meeting of committee members who, somewhat nonplussed, debated the matter against a background of adjacent hubbub. First, it appears, they suggested Lillywhite should continue as umpire and that Willsher's bowling action be overlooked for the rest of the match. Lillywhite, for his part, quite understandably rejected such a proposal and offered to resign rather than go back on his decision, adding that he had merely enforced the law and, moreover, had warned Willsher before no-balling him. In the end, the committee declared their confidence in Lillywhite and assured him that his future with the county club would not be

Fateful match at The Oval in August 1862. Umpire John Lillywhite (far left) no-balled Edgar Willsher (alongside him), almost causing a riot – Caesar himself sometimes needed little provocation to put up his fists – and precipitating the legislation that freed bowlers to raise their arms above the horizontal.

affected. Even so, it was deemed prudent to appoint another umpire (George Street) to take over.

Willsher and Lillywhite soon became friends again, but some players felt less forgiving and were unable to concede that the Surrey club were all sweetness and light. It was widely believed in the North that Lillywhite had been specially engaged to no-ball Willsher, whose bowling action in that contentious over was generally considered to be no more suspect than normal. Caffyn, who played in the match, had this to say: 'There is no doubt that Willsher was in the habit of bowling above the shoulder, but then so were nine out of ten bowlers at that time. The old law was an absurd one, and one wonders why it should have remained in force as long as it did.'

The episode had served to underline to MCC that a major clause in the laws needed urgent revision. However, almost two years elapsed before the governing body gave its official blessing to overarm bowling or, as R.S.Rait Kerr put it in his *The Laws of Cricket*, before MCC 'finally surrendered by granting complete emancipation to the bowlers'.

Although the Oval incident helped to expedite the new law, it unhappily added to the differences between Surrey CCC and northern professionals. Surrey played Cambridgeshire in 1862 for the last time until 1871, reportedly because of 'disputes and jealousies in the cricketing world'. Matches between Surrey and Nottinghamshire were proven crowd-pullers but, owing to an 'unfortunate hitch', those counties did not meet in 1863.

Correspondence columns in newspapers reflected the growing acerbity. Some irate contributors harked back to the unpleasantness surrounding the selection of the side to tour Australia the previous year and accused 'certain individuals' of trying to disrupt the Surrey club. Although wild allegations and thinly veiled euphemisms exaggerated and aggravated the situation, there was no denying the friction that existed between the rival groups of players and clubs. An abrasive nick was fast developing into a festering sore.

The bad feeling further manifested itself during the 1863 season when Parr and others refused to turn out for The North against Surrey at Manchester in August. Their absence did not prevent The North from winning but the team's managers, while admitting difficulties in raising a side, declared they were 'not solely reliant upon a particular division to supply an eleven to represent the North'. Brave words, but it was the end of the fixture for years.

Shortly after that match, Caesar was with the All-England XI at Durdham Downs, Clifton, playing for the first time against a man who would revolutionise cricket. To describe W.G.Grace just then as 'a man' is to age him prematurely, for he had only recently celebrated his 15th birthday. He was one of four Graces in the Twenty-Two of Bristol and District and, thanks largely to that family's efforts, the AEE crumbled to an innings defeat. One wonders how Caesar then rated the tall lad who calmly stroked 32 off some class bowlers.

That season marked the end of Caesar's playing association with the All-England XI, for whom he had appeared regularly since 1851. It is possible his departure from the side, now dominated by northern players, had something to do with the prickly relationships at that time and there was, too, the hint of a new touring team being formed by southerners.

In view of the sensitive climate, it must have been an agreeable surprise to find that a truly representative England party could be selected to go to Australia without the furore that had attended the one in 1861. This visit also provided for a sortie into New Zealand. The twelve were: George Parr, captain, Alfred Clarke, John Jackson and Cris Tinley (Nottinghamshire); Julius Caesar, William Caffyn and Tom Lockyer (Surrey); Tom Hayward, Bob Carpenter and George Tarrant (Cambridgeshire); George Anderson (Yorkshire); and the only amateur, E.M. Grace. The side (average age 31) was to complete a programme of 16 matches against numerical odds without conceding defeat.

After a champagne lunch at the Adelphi Hotel, Liverpool, the players went to the city's docks where they were cheered by a large crowd of wellwishers. It was October 15. They sailed in *Great Britain,* arriving to an enthusiastic welcome in Melbourne on December 16.

Two days before Christmas a poem, 'The Australian Twelve', appeared in *The Sporting Life.* It included these lines:

Among this hitting class, and greatly famed,
The Surrey Caesar (Julius) may be named;
And, if that enemy of his, the gout,
Is not inclined to trouble him while out,
To see him bat will be a glorious treat,
So lively is his play, and yet so neat.

Chapter Eleven

Touring the Antipodes

A crowd estimated at 20,000 gathered at the Melbourne ground on New Year's Day 1864 for England's opening game of the tour, against Twenty-Two of Victoria who, according to *The Leader*, were proud to submit 'their colonial metal to the test of the imperial standard'.

Many of the spectators reclined in seats beneath the three tri-coloured domes of a big grandstand. Members chatted in the garden-fronted pavilion. The ladies' marquee was packed and a temporary stand filled to capacity. People perched in trees overlooking the ground, and the 'shilling reserve on the hill' was very well patronised, while the majority of onlookers stood ringing the arena, the boundary of which was marked by red flags set at regular intervals along a chain fence.

The sun beat down from a clear sky, bunting fluttered, tents flapped gently in a light breeze – a memorable scene for the visiting cricketers. Young elms planted by the previous tourists were flourishing, a newspaper reporter writing that the 'appearance of the men's patronymics at the stems served to remind strangers that their names are still familiar in our ears as household words'. To help spectators identify the players, scorecards bore printed colours matching sashes affixed to white helmets worn by the Englishmen, whose neat attire also included red-spotted shirts. The advanced 'telegraph' gave not only the current score, but also the names of batsmen in prominent lettering.

The pitch and closely-cropped outfield were in excellent order and, batting first, the home side totalled 146 against 'the flower of English cricketry'. Not without a lot of application, England made 176 (Caesar, opening the innings, scored 2) and, having then got rid of the Victorians for 143, were thus left 114 to win in about three hours. It did not appear to be an unduly onerous task but Tarrant and Grace were out cheaply and, with little over 30 on the board, Hayward was run out, which was greeted by 'loud cheering and throwing up of hats'. England had proceeded to 106 for 4 when stumps were drawn so precisely at six o'clock that there arose 'some little show of dissatisfaction on the part of some of the people present'.

Caesar proved to be a welcome tourist. His puckish sense of humour,

The 1863-64 English team which toured Australia: standing: Julius Caesar, Alfred Clarke, George Tarrant, George Parr (captain), E.M. Grace, Robert Carpenter, George Anderson, Billy Caffyn; on steps: Cris Tinley, Tom Lockyer, Tom Hayward, John Jackson. The figure in the top-hat is thought to be J.H. Dark, proprietor of Lord's ground.

liking for a pint, unpretentious manner and adventurous batting would have appealed to Australians. He was called upon to say a few words at functions where other speakers could not resist comparing his own 'invasion' and 'conquest' with those of the noble Roman emperor. Although he doubtless laughed with the rest, such references must have palled after a while.

England's campaign continued with matches in a region noted for its goldfields. The first was at Back Creek, Sandhurst, where flooding followed baking temperatures had combined to make the ground rock-hard and virtually grassless. The surface suited 'Spider' Tinley, who spread his web to take 26 wickets for 57 in his side's win over Twenty-Two of Bendigo. The tourists then coasted to victory over twenty-two locals at Ballarat by an innings and 12 runs, Caesar making the game's top score of 40. England also won resoundingly at both Ararat and Maryborough before sailing to New Zealand, a country in which the European settlers were still skirmishing with the native Maoris.

The Englishmen experienced no difficulty in recording easy wins over twenty-twos in Otago, Canterbury and Christchurch although the chasm in standards was narrowed, to some extent, by the poor state of the pitches. At one ground, the strip looked 'in no way fit for cricket', so a fresh one was cut – almost at right-angles to the original.

Julius Caesar's most exciting moment in New Zealand had nothing to do with cricket. He and his colleagues were horse-riding along a high track overlooking the sea at Lyttelton, near Christchurch, when his mount turned 'rusty' and galloped down the steep slope. The others watched in horror and Caesar blanched when he realised the danger of being hurled, with or without steed, to the rocky beach hundreds of feet below. Fortunately, the animal came to a halt just short of the edge and allowed itself to be ridden back to the path.

After the last match in New Zealand, in Dunedin, the England players indulged in some athletic challenges, in one of which Caesar easily beat Caffyn over 100 yards. The happy England party returned to Australia at the end of February – an eight-day voyage – and, after inflicting an innings defeat on Twenty-Two of Castlemaine, moved on to Sydney and another generous reception. Nearly 20,000 people were at the ground on March 16 for the heralded match with Twenty-Two of New South Wales which, because of frequent interruptions by rain, the tourists eventually won eight days later! Bad weather also interfered with the return game, which was left undecided.

Yet a third meeting between the two sides began on April 2 and England came perilously close to being beaten. Having dismissed New South Wales for 68, they were surprisingly shot out for only 75. Bowlers remained in command and the Twenty-Two totalled 83 in their second innings, leaving England to make 77 runs to win. The NSW team included Charles Lawrence, who had stayed in Sydney to coach after the 1862 tour, and his bowling (10 for 46 in the match) almost led to the downfall of his own countrymen. Starting the last day at 18 for 2, England certainly found it hard going and the scores were level when last-man Tinley joined Lockyer amid 'indescribable excitement'. There was a despairing groan from the crowd when Tinley offered a simple chance to mid-on, who dropped it and wished

The English cricketers exhibit their skills before a good attendance on the public expanse of the Domain in Sydney.

his name wasn't Curtis as the ball trickled away and the Englishmen scrambled the winning run.

Excitement of a much more startling nature occurred the following day when the steamer *Wonga Wonga*, in which the tourists were sailing back to Melbourne and barely two hours out of Sydney, collided with the brigantine *Viceroy*, which sank within five minutes. Happily, all hands were saved, but *Wonga Wonga*, minus bowsprit and with damaged headgear, had to return to harbour. Most players were enjoying an evening meal when the accident happened in 'dark and hazy' conditions. Food and crockery leapt from the tables and, according to Caffyn, poor George Parr was 'utterly dazed and paralysed with alarm' while Tarrant 'quite lost his head'. Living up to his nickname 'Tear'Em', the young man rushed below to grab his collection of curios and then tried to get into a boat being lowered to rescue the skipper and crew from the doomed brigantine. He was equally firmly pushed back by the sailors, who told him in unvarnished terms to make himself scarce.

The whole experience was very frightening, however. Shouts echoed in the gloom, some women passengers became over-wrought, but amid all the confusion it appears that Julius Caesar remained calm, helped the seamen as best he could and behaved in a 'manner worthy of his name'. Unperturbed by the whole drama was 'Foghorn' Jackson who, having partaken liberally of a farewell luncheon in Sydney, went on snoring contentedly in his bunk.

The team eventually arrived in Melbourne on April 11 and rounded off their programme with matches in that area. In a pick-up game Caesar was given a bowl and duly celebrated the rare chance by taking 9 for 49 in the match. Bob Carpenter made the tour's highest score when he carted the Ballarat bowling for 121 and finished with the best batting aggregate of 400 runs. Caffyn decided to stay in Australia, accepting an offer from Melbourne Cricket Club to be coach, at an annual salary of £300. He later moved to Sydney to take up a similar post and divided his time between that and his bread-and-butter job of hairdressing. When he finally returned to his homeland in 1871, he would find a very different cricket scene.

A few weeks after the other successful tourists got back to England, a rangy youngster walked out to bat for the South Wales Club against the Surrey club at The Oval. William Gilbert Grace, the fourth son of a Downend doctor, was then just short of his 16th birthday and, apart from his tender years, his impact on that game was not sensational. Within days, however, he was battering the bowling of the Sussex Gentlemen at Hove for 170 and 56 not out. From that moment, cricket would never be quite the same again. The Gloucestershire boy was to become the greatest batsman ever seen, a long-reigning monarch from whom, in the eyes of the many privileged to watch him, the crown was never wrested.

In the same way as a searing summer or withering winter can upset the balance of nature, so Grace disturbed the equipoise of cricket. Throughout the history of the game there had been players who significantly tilted the scales in favour of bat or ball, but somehow they seemed quite human by comparison. Most of his contemporaries could but strive modestly in his majestic shadow. Here was an incredible new force of outstanding ability and presence who would transform the whole image of the game and increasingly dominate its stage during the rest of Julius Caesar's lifetime and for many years beyond.

Chapter Twelve

Sweet and Sour

Julius Caesar was now 34 and still highly rated, but heading towards the veteran stage. At The Oval, fresh faces advanced to be recognised. Tom Humphrey and Harry Jupp, the 'Young Stonewall', were becoming a regular opening partnership which would serve Surrey well during most of the 1860s. Then there was Ted Pooley, who in 1868 would set a wicketkeeping record of 12 dismissals in a match (eight caught and four stumped), unequalled until the Australian, Don Tallon, also got a dozen – 71 years later. James Street was also making a name as a fast bowler. With such talent around, Caesar needed a big score to help consolidate his position.

A sea-specked breeze blew lightly across the sunlit Royal Brunswick ground at Hove on July 18, 1864 when Sussex and Surrey started a three-day match. A sizeable crowd spread themselves around the pleasant arena and watched the home side total 213, of which Payne and Stubberfield put on 65 for the last wicket. Caesar had distinguished himself with a smart pick-up at midwicket to run out F.F.Thomas which, said *Bell's Life*, was a 'masterpiece of cricket'. Indeed, Caesar's quick reflexes had always served him well in the field and he often stood at point. In one game, the ball grazed his hip as it flashed towards the boundary from the fierce bat of the Hon.C.G.Lyttelton. 'That cut ought to be preserved in a glass case,' remarked Julius with relief and admiration.

Jupp and Humphrey began the Surrey reply and had put on exactly 100 by the end of the first day. The pair added 13 the next morning before Humphrey, looking to loft the ball over the English Channel, was bowled for 60. Jupp went on to reach 71 and, although Mortlock managed to stay, there was a partial collapse and half the wickets were down for 185.

Caesar immediately opened his account with a sweep for five, and during the afternoon treated the spectators to an array of fine strokes. Runs flowed as surely as the tide not far away and he and Mortlock, who made 69, put on 110 for the sixth wicket. Caesar went on to complete his century amid loud applause, though he may not have done so but for some luck which favoured James Street, with whom he shared an eighth-wicket partnership of 91.

Street, who got 31, had two narrow escapes. He was beaten by a ball that dislodged a bail from its groove but did not fall and later skyed a shot to midwicket 'which was a chance to Mr Hale, but missing it he unfortunately got it in the mouth instead'.

Tom Sewell and William Shepherd also contributed tailend support and when the innings closed at 419, Caesar remained undefeated on 132, including a five and 10 fours – the highest score of his life. *Bell's Life* declared they could not praise Caesar too much and his batting showed 'he has all his cricket still in him, the bowling being quite up to the mark'. In the opinion of the *Sussex Express*, it was 'as finely a played and truly artistic innings as we have had the pleasure of witnessing for a very long time. A complete ovation awaited this fine exponent of the batting art on his return to the dressing-room'. Caesar duly received talent money for his performance and Surrey went on to win by an innings and 54 runs.

Regrettably, the 1864 season was marred by further bickering among professionals and this reached a head in September. During the match at Islington, where The South trounced The North, a number of whose stars would not appear, a resolution signed by 13 southerners, including Caesar, announced: 'We, the South of England, decline playing at Newmarket on October 6th, 7th and 8th, as they, the North of England, refused to play in London'. A sulky, childish tit-for-tat on the face of it, but emotions obviously ran deep and the fixture planned for Newmarket was replaced by another featuring a combined Cambridgeshire and Yorkshire side against Kent and Nottinghamshire.

There was a much happier atmosphere at the Broadwater ground on September 12 when hundreds turned up to watch the testimonial match for Caesar organised by his fellow townsmen. Tom Lockyer had been similarly honoured in Croydon after his return from the Australian tour, a gesture which prompted the *West Surrey Times* to ask: 'What does Godalming think of doing for her brave Julius Caesar?' The great day had arrived. The South-Western Railway Company offered half-price return fares on the three days of the game, during the intervals of which the band of the 2nd Surrey Militia played popular tunes in 'admirable style'. Arrangements for the occasion were worthy of the 'universal esteem' in which the player was held and, the *Surrey Advertiser* added, 'what Robin Hood was to archery, so is such a man as Julius Caesar to cricketing'.

Billy Mortlock and Tom Lockyer skippered sides which included most of the Surrey team and a few Sussex men. The weather, sadly no respecter of grand events, failed to fulfil its early promise and the match was frequently interrupted by rain. For the record, Lockyer's XI (109 and 160 for 6) gained a substantial moral victory, Mortlock's team being dispatched for a paltry 40 in their only innings. There was no play after half-past two on the final day when a downpour sent people scurrying for shelter.

That evening, many wellwishers assembled for the presentation to Caesar of a gold watch with a 'massive' Albert chain and a purse of sovereigns. Their hero was much praised for bringing honour to Godalming by virtue of his feats at cricket and as a 'straightforward and upright man'. There was 'loud and long cheering' for Caesar, who said it had always been his motto to 'go straight', and although it was difficult for cricketers in the public eye not to make some enemies, he had not done so and, moreover, had made many friends. He tactfully refrained from mentioning the current disharmony between professionals but the meeting's chairman, Murray Marshall, did refer briefly, but significantly, to the proposed formation of the United South of England XI.

In fact, the 'Eleven' was duly inaugurated in London on November 17 with Edgar Willsher as secretary. Other founder-members included Caesar, Bennett, Jupp, Humphrey, Mortlock, Lockyer, John Lillywhite, James Lillywhite (junior), Griffith, Sewell, H.H.Stephenson, Pooley, H.H.Ellis and Tom Hearne. Because of this new organisation, the United All-England XI lost all their southern players. 'The mischief,' as *The Sporting Life* called it, 'has been long brewing and various causes into which we shall not enter have from time to time widened the breach between the North and South men.' Despite the hammer-blow, the UAEE decided to continue with an all-northern complement. The secession of the southerners, first from the All-England XI and then from the United All-England XI, plus a growing demand for county cricket, effectively put an end to the great days of those famous travelling teams born of a venture by William Clarke 20 years earlier.

Unhappy relationships were further soured at The Oval on July 15, 1865, the final day of a very grim struggle between Surrey and Nottinghamshire. An incident sparked off much resentment and recrimination at such a sensitive time when even minor differences, fanned by frustration and suspicion, were seized upon by rival factions to raise the temperature. The Surrey club were already in bad odour with some northern professionals, not least George Parr, who declined to appear at The Oval. Even so,

Nottinghamshire sent down a strong side for this game, with high hopes of repeating their victory over the southern county at Trent Bridge the previous month.

It proved a hard-fought battle and Surrey were left to make 195 in their second innings to win. They found it tough going, particularly against Jemmy Grundy, who clean bowled Jupp, Humphrey and Pooley, had Mortlock caught and then got rid of Caesar. Only Stephenson really defied Grundy, who took the first nine wickets, and 'HH' was 75 not out when last-man Sewell joined him. Fourteen runs were still required and, somewhat surprisingly, Sewell got the lot. It was during those dramatic closing overs, however, that Nottinghamshire tempers rose with the score.

Sewell survived a confident appeal for leg-before off the very first ball he received. The fielders looked aggrieved and their displeasure mounted as he sneaked eight runs. Then he missed a ball from 'Foghorn' Jackson and wicketkeeper Sam Biddulph put down the stumps. There was a loud, triumphant appeal and Biddulph, 'naturally considering the game was over', stuffed the ball into his pocket and, surrounded by jubilant colleagues, walked towards the dressing-room. They were called back by George Lee, the Surrey umpire, who informed them that Sewell was not out.

The crowd cheered as the batsmen stole another single. With only 10 minutes to go, five runs were still needed and Sewell struck them with one resounding blow. He was hoisted high by delighted supporters and carried to the Oval pavilion, while the incensed Notts fielders angrily left the field convinced that Sewell had been properly stumped, one of them, William Oscroft, contending that he was out by 'a yard and a half'. An exaggeration, perhaps, but the mood of the visiting team can be imagined. They felt cheated out of victory.

Unpleasant exchanges ensued, and the chance taken by members of both teams to 'rake up old sores'. It was asserted by some that Lee had been greatly influenced by sections of the crowd who roared 'Not out!', while others commended the umpire for his fair and courageous decision. Damage had been done, however, and there were no more matches between the two counties for three years. The *Nottingham Daily Guardian*, whose account of the controversy was based on statements by four fielders and 'some gentlemen who had the opportunity of speaking to both Surrey and Notts men after the match', came out with a scalding attack on the Surrey club: 'All hopes of healing the breach between Surrey and the northern counties appear now to have vanished and the inevitable character of unfairness with which that county and all connected with it has long possessed must be taken as indelibly fixed.'

Nottinghamshire were not alone in that antipathy. When Surrey had played at Bramall Lane in June, five Yorkshiremen (George Anderson, George Atkinson, Roger Iddison, Joseph Rowbotham and Edward Stephenson) refused to appear against them. The dissenting quintet also declined to take part in the return match at The Oval in August – the last fixture between the counties for two seasons. Arthur Haygarth, compiler of *Cricket Scores and Biographies*, duly observed: 'Altogether this match (as well as others these last few years at The Oval) was a good deal spoiled by the continued disputes in the professional cricketing community. It is also to be regretted that whatsoever the quarrels between cricketers might be, they should prevent any from assisting their counties.'

Despite such current distractions, Julius Caesar batted well for Surrey during that 1865 season, with a top score of 82 against Hampshire and three others over fifty – 74 against Cambridge University, 55 off the Middlesex bowlers and 66 not out against Sussex, made 'in his brilliant hitting style'. He totalled 573 runs from 23 innings and scores in other games, mostly for the United South of England, brought his aggregate to more than 800. He also took 19 catches – the most in county matches that season. Caesar was in form and his forthright approach to batting was as popular as ever with the crowds.

Then, a disastrous split-second started an agonising decline.

Chapter Thirteen

The Fatal Moment

It was shortly before 11 o'clock on the morning of Wednesday, October 18, 1865. Rain fell on Munstead Heath, elevated land a mile or so to the south-east of Godalming, giving the trees a dark sheen and binding fallen leaves into a soggy carpet. Shots rang out as pheasants were flushed from cover.

Walking slowly across the saturated ground and accompanied by the gamekeeper were Lieutenant-Colonel Frederick Marshall, his elder brother, Murray, a visiting friend, Richard Dickenson, and Julius Caesar, regarded as an experienced and reliable marksman. The party had just entered a small field when an incident of the 'most distressing nature' occurred.

As one of the beaters, 45-year-old William Foster, started to work a hedge, a gun went off and the charge of shot smashed into his back. A trail of smoke extended from Caesar about six yards behind. He was heard to exclaim: 'Oh God, what have I done?'

The stricken man, whose injuries were to prove fatal, was carried on a hurdle to a nearby cottage and a messenger hurried to the town to summon medical aid. Meanwhile, everything possible was done to alleviate suffering and to staunch bleeding from a very extensive wound, although a mortified Caesar could not help much because he was so frightened. Dr Balchin arrived, tended to Foster for three hours and arranged to return later, but 'scarcely anticipated' seeing him alive again. That evening, the doctor and Caesar set off in a fly for the cottage only to learn on the way that the beater had died.

'I never saw any man in such a state as Julius Caesar was when we heard of Foster's death,' Dr Balchin declared at the inquest held two days later at the Royal Oak, Hascombe. 'He sobbed like a child and was dreadfully agitated by the intelligence.' He also told the West Surrey coroner, C.J.Woods, that he considered death ensued from 'exhaustion and shock to the nervous system'.

Richard Dickenson testified that he understood Caesar had put his gun under his arm to protect it from the rain and it was possible the strap of his shot-pouch touched the trigger. He dropped the gun immediately after it fired.

Coroner: Was Caesar much agitated?
Dickenson: I shall never forget his look of agony.
Coroner: So early in the morning, it is scarcely necessary to ask you the question, but I must – was Caesar sober?
Dickenson: Perfectly sober. The gun was, I imagine, on full cock. It was the right-hand barrel which exploded. So far as my observation can go, I am satisfied the explosion resulted from an accident. I am confident from the conduct and demeanour of Julius Caesar after the accident that it was the subject of intense mortification for him.

Thomas Cousens, a gamekeeper in the employ of Colonel Marshall, said he remained with Foster until his death and, although conscious until then, he never commented on the accident or mentioned Caesar's name. Cousens said he found the gun to be in perfect order and also confirmed the sobriety of the shooting party. Neither he nor Colonel Marshall, of the 2nd Life Guards, who also gave evidence, could shed any real light on why the gun went off. Marshall deposed that he had shot with Caesar for many years and thought he was 'the most careful man with a gun I have ever been out with'.

Julius Caesar, who was 'much affected' when giving his testimony, stated that he had owned the gun for seven or eight years and it was in excellent working order. He recalled that when he came over a bank into the meadow he put the hammers down from full to half-cock but, thinking it possible a pheasant might get up, he again cocked the gun. As it was raining, he tucked it under his arm.

Coroner: Are you able to explain how it went off?
Caesar: I am perfectly unable to do so. I wore a shot-pouch and possibly the strap touched the trigger, but I felt nothing so that I cannot account for it. I have carried my gun a thousand times in the same way. The gun went off and that is all I can say.

After summing-up the evidence, the coroner said he felt sure the jury would relieve Caesar from any imputation, culpability or carelessness. It seemed a mystery as to why the gun went off, but it was clearly accidental. He was sorry to learn that William Foster had left a wife and seven children unprovided for and was certain the jury would sympathise with them and also with Caesar, who had been the 'innocent destroyer of this poor man's life'.

The jury expressed similar sentiments after formally returning a verdict of 'Accidental Death' and the foreman handed their fees, amounting to 12 shillings, to Colonel Marshall for the benefit of the deceased's family.

The whole harrowing experience became indelibly fused in Caesar's thoughts and, in the view of Caffyn, he 'never got over the shock till the day of his death'. Despite exoneration from all blame, he could not really forgive himself. In reviewing Caesar's batting in the previous season, *The Sporting Life* advanced the hope that 'this much-respected player will not allow the painful circumstances of a few months ago to affect his cricket, as we should be very sorry indeed to lose the pleasure of recording the doings of the popular Julius, esteemed as he is by all with whom he comes into contact'.

Nevertheless, he was to give up playing in the first-class game after stumbling through only two more seasons.

Chapter Fourteen

The Game is Done

Julius Caesar struggled vainly in 1866 to recapture form. His 22 innings for Surrey (one fewer than in 1865) produced a mere 247 runs, while in 19 visits to the crease for the United South of England XI he managed only 84. The contrast with his fine batting the previous season was too striking to be ascribed to a bad patch or rotten luck. There can be precious little doubt that the effects of the shooting tragedy weighed heavily on his heart and mind.

Meanwhile, other problems beset a divided cricket world. Thirteen northern professionals refused to appear with southerners in the Gentlemen v Players match, whereupon MCC decided that all players in matches at Lord's be chosen from 'those who are willing to play together in a friendly manner in the matches on that ground'.

The schism had also been debated at the annual meeting of Surrey CCC. One member demanded to know from the committee, who, he said, 'must be aware of the reason', exactly why George Parr had not played at The Oval since 1859 and why, for the past three seasons, other principal northern players had also boycotted the ground. He pointed out, moreover, that recent letters in newspapers questioned the conduct of both the secretary and the club.

Henry Marshall, the president, said he was unaware that the club had given offence and was convinced they had done nothing to provoke the split. The secretary, William Burrup, then offered to resign if members felt he was an obstacle to northern professionals or had in any way exceeded his duties (cries of 'No'). Giving his version of the affair in 1861 when Mallam arrived to arrange the tour to Australia, Burrup claimed that Parr was not only rude to the visitor but also believed that he (Burrup) prevented his going. Burrup denied pushing forward H.H.Stephenson as captain and repudiated any suggestion that he unfairly chose a majority of Surrey men. It was only after certain northerners declined to go, he asserted, that most of the southern players were invited. Members reaffirmed their confidence in Burrup as secretary, only three out of more than a hundred indicating dissent.

Matters did not end there, of course. Angry letters flowed into the Press, contributors ranging themselves behind Burrup or Parr and hurling fresh spanners into the controversial works. The mud flew. *The Sporting Life* eventually decided enough was enough and closed its correspondence columns to 'this disagreeable question'. The newspaper added: 'If the northern men will not play on the Surrey ground – and we presume they are determined not to do so – we think there is no object to be gained in continually bringing these grievances before the public, who must be sick of the whole affair and who, in the ensuing season, will doubtless go where they can see the best cricket for their money, without reference to Messrs Parr, Burrup or anybody else.'

Surrey had little cause for jubilation on the field either, winning only five of their 14 matches in 1866. After crushing defeats by Kent, Sussex and then by Middlesex within the space of a fortnight, they began a three-day game against England on July 30 and fared even worse, losing by an innings and 296 runs. The chief reason for their abject discomfort was W.G.Grace, then just 12 days past his 18th birthday, who struck the first of his 126 centuries in first-class cricket. In fact, he made a double-hundred (224 not out) – then the highest individual score seen at The Oval. Grace's wonderful display provided Caesar with a glorious page for his scrapbook of cricket memories, although his own scores were somewhat less impressive – 0 and 3.

The 1867 season, Caesar's last in top cricket, hinted a slight thaw in the icy relationship between north and south. Emerging from relative isolation, Yorkshire twice beat Surrey, against whom Iddison and Rowbotham turned out but Anderson, Stephenson and Atkinson did not. The overall situation remained delicate, however, and some Cambridgeshire men took umbrage because the Sheffield committee had promoted the Yorkshire v Surrey game at Bramall Lane in June and would not themselves appear in a match with Yorkshire scheduled for July 8, thus forcing the fixture to be cancelled. It all seemed rather churlish.

Caesar played little cricket that year because of attacks of gout, an extremely painful disease causing swollen joints, not helped by rich food or alcohol and requiring complete rest. In May, he appeared four times (twice each for Surrey and the United South) and then umpired in several matches before returning to the county side on August 12 when Middlesex visited The Oval. 'Julius Caesar's appearance in flannel,' wrote one loyal journalist, 'was evidently pleasing to the lookers-on and a little bit of good cricket the Godalming man played.' The operative word surely was 'little', for he made

THE GAME IS DONE

only 2 in his first innings and was bowled first ball by Hearne in his second. Two weeks later, Julius Caesar made his swansong for Surrey in a drawn game against Lancashire at Old Trafford. No storybook finish attended his departure; he was run out for 1 and, in his second knock, got another single before being stumped. His seven innings for Surrey in 1867 yielded a mere four runs. So, with a mild whimper and not a bang, ended his county career extending over 19 seasons. He was 37.

Apart from just one more appearance (and a duck) for the United South, Caesar saw out the season in a judicial role. He umpired in Tom Lockyer's benefit match at The Oval, where England beat Surrey by nine wickets, and also in mid-September when the United South met Nineteen of Godalming. The latter game was at 'beautiful' Broadwater from where, said the *Surrey Standard,* the 'glorious Surrey hills that surround the ground, when gilded by the sunbeams, were seen to the very best advantage'. The match attracted 'one of the largest assemblages of all classes seen at the ground for many years', according to *The Sporting Life,* and was notable for a remarkable spell of lob bowling by 19-year-old Walter Baptist Money (captain of the Harrow XI and shortly to shine at Cambridge University). He took all 10 of the South's wickets in one innings for 66 runs.

Caesar's last season with Surrey coincided with the retirement from the presidency of Henry Marshall, who had held office for 11 years during which time the club had greatly expanded. The recent years had been trying enough but, in his farewell speech, he was able to point to the encouraging fact that the 1868 fixture list would once more include Nottinghamshire. His nephew, Colonel Frederick Marshall, succeeded him.

Surrey organised a benefit match for Caesar – 'one of the most civil fellows and all-round cricketers who ever took the field,' commented *Lillywhite's Cricketer's Companion* – and it took place at The Oval on August 17, 18, 19, 1868, when a combined Surrey-Middlesex side met England. Some very fine players accepted invitations, among them W.G.Grace, Edgar Willsher, V.E.Walker, C.I.Thornton, Sam Biddulph and his 24-year-old Nottinghamshire colleague, George Summers, a very promising batsman. (Sadly, he would die two years later after being struck on the head by a ball at Lord's.) England lost an exciting, if low-scoring, game by one wicket in unfriendly weather and Caesar was the richer by nearly £400.

The *Surrey Gazette* recalled it was 'now some 24 years ago that the

Godalming people became conscious that they had amongst them a rising youth whose prowess with the willow and whose skill at the wicket was something above the average'. The paper added that the shooting incident 'completely unnerved him and destroyed much of that quickness of eye and alertness so essential to all good cricketers. He again entered the field, but after 20 years of active service he had done in the cause of cricket had begun to tell upon him and leave those marks which so clearly tell us that youth and energy cannot last forever.'

Chapter Fifteen

Times of Torment

Although still a comparatively young man, Julius Caesar aged appreciably after that fateful day on Munstead Heath. Tormenting memories, his subsequent retirement from first-class cricket, in which he had shone so brightly, and the mental adjustment to a less glamorous existence undoubtedly took their toll.

Caesar maintained links with the game he loved, however. He umpired in a number of important matches every season until 1875 and once, in August 1872, at Hove, where Surrey won by two wickets, he caused 'much unpleasant excitement' by ruling that H.R.J.Charlwood (Sussex), then on 73, was out 'hit ball twice'. From time to time, he played for sides in his home town and among the founder-members of the Broadwater Club in 1867 were Caesar and James Street, who, for some years, was landlord of the Row Barge Inn in Bridge Street.

Caesar appears to have given up carpentry, entirely or partially, to run his own business selling cricket gear, the *Godalming Directory* of 1867 (and later editions) listing him as: 'Caesar, Julius; Ockford Road, cricketing outfitter'. The 1871 census returns show he was still living at that address with his wife and their three sons.

The removal of Charterhouse School from London to Godalming in June 1872 was a culminating triumph of determination, organisation and diplomacy for the headmaster, the Revd William Haig Brown, and also a red-letter day for local tradesmen. The new buildings stood above the town like a sturdy sentinel, turrets and pinnacles thrusting upwards to form an impressive silhouette against the sky. The school required a cricket professional not only to coach the boys but also to supervise the maintenance of the ground. Julius Caesar got the job as well as an agreement to supply 'all the requisite materials for the game'.

A fortnight after the move from London, the School XI drew a match with Godalming at Broadwater. The *Surrey Gazette* generously predicted the boys would 'prove no despicable opponents to any eleven that may be brought against them', but qualified the praise after the return match three weeks later when it felt the lads had yet to learn the art of defence. 'Rapid scoring is only desirable when it accompanies a safe wicket,' the writer advised, 'and Julius Caesar will doubtless take care to inculcate its application to the pupils he has to coach.'

The newspaper also said the Charterhouse ground looked as 'level as a billiard table' but *Bell's Life*, less easily impressed perhaps, thought the soil was too sandy and in need of 'a plentiful top dressing ere it can claim to be called a cricket ground'. Moreover, it believed that Caesar could not be expected 'to turn out a good eleven until it is possible for the boys to play fast as well as slow bowling on the practice wickets'. Caesar received an honourable mention in a letter written by the headmaster's wife to her parents in July 1872. It referred to her small daughter's birthday gifts including the 'long talked-of and thought-of doves have just arrived, procured for me by Julius Caesar who is now Cricket Coach to Charterhouse – Umpire – and Presider in general over matches – Cricket Ground'.

Julius occasionally took part in domestic school matches, an example being in June 1873 when he and James Street, who would himself be coach there, assisted The Masters against The School. The fact that Caesar hit 53 not out in their first innings of 97 and then 32 out of 62 in their second, as well as taking four of the five wickets to fall in the boys' second knock, enhanced his own status. It also suggests that the masters were not so much 'assisted' as rescued from humiliation. Caesar's association with Charterhouse lasted four years. For the Past v Present game on July 1, 1875, the *Surrey Advertiser* noted that he had prepared an 'excellent' wicket and that the tidy state of the ground reflected 'much credit' upon him.

For all that, Julius was a saddened man and probably suffering from indifferent health at the time. A year earlier (July 24, 1874) his wife, Jane, had died from cancer at the age of 45 and the loss 'told upon him greatly'. He more than likely appeared strained and somewhat preoccupied, was still plagued by gout and possibly had the beginnings of heart trouble.

He would surely have derived some comfort and fatherly pride from the cricketing ability of his sons, however. Frederick Sankey Caesar, the eldest and a 25-year-old accountant when he was married at the church of his baptism on November 28, 1875, was a useful club player and probably the 'F.Caesar', secretary for a time of Godalming CC after its resuscitation in 1871. While the 13-year-old Benjamin had yet to prove himself, the son most likely to make it as a top player was Julius, junior. He played in the local matches, fast developing into a very good all-rounder, and had been engaged as an assistant professional at Charterhouse for the 1876 season – destined to be his father's last at the public school.

The younger Julius, who celebrated his 17th birthday on August 7, had a highly-strung temperament, however, and was also very confused and frightened. His love affair with a publican's daughter, then living in Guildford, led to her becoming pregnant. The poor youth was petrified with dilemma and fear. He received a letter from the girl (dated September 27) asking him in effect what his intentions were, and, as a result, he went to see her. During the evening of Monday, October 2, the couple visited a fair at St Catherine's Hill, Guildford, before strolling near the railway line, where she left him at about 20 minutes before 10 o'clock.

Early the next morning, a platelayer came across Julius's mutilated body on the main-line track between Peasmarsh and Compton bridges – almost equidistant from Godalming and Guildford. In the boy's coat pocket was a lock of his girlfriend's hair, a letter from 'Your fond lover, Laura Whittle', and another marked 'Private' and headed 'Guildford, October 2nd 1876', addressed to 'Julius Caesar, senior, Godalming', which read as follows:

My dear father – I can't bear to think for what I have done and to think what a bother I have been to you lately. So I am determined to do a thing, which a good many will miss me after I am gone, especially one, my dear Laura Whittle. I can't think what will become of her. I have ruined the poor girl. I should like you to send all my things that are in my drawer to her, as she is the only one who will do anything for me. Don't let Fred know. I am sick and tired of this life. I should have done it a long time ago only for one reason; I thought of the one who loves me dearly. What would poor mother say if she were alive. Never mind, don't fret. Oh, I can't bear to think what a blackguard I have been in my time. Good bye. God bless you. From your unfaithful son, Julius Caesar.

It was a poignant and guilt-ridden farewell. William Brewser, an uncle, told the inquest at the Parrot Inn, Shalford, the next day that the boy had been absent from home since the previous Saturday, but was on the 'very best terms' with his father. From childhood he had been excitable and very nervous, would not go to bed without a light and even when older refused to enter a room in the dark. Police Constable Edgeler gave evidence that he had seen the crushed body face downward on the line shortly after six o'clock the previous morning. One leg had been severed and was lying about seven yards away. John Debenham, the solicitor representing the Caesar family, said the boy's father could not attend because he was 'completely prostrated' by the news.

Summing up, the West Surrey Coroner, George H.Hull, declared that young Julius had apparently become 'afraid of his father hearing of the position he was in and the idea of getting married at the early age of seventeen evidently upset him'. The jury returned a verdict to the effect that the lad had 'committed suicide while labouring under temporary insanity'.

Chapter Sixteen

Darkly Fades the Twilight

A lready burdened by other tragic memories, Julius Caesar suffered acutely after his son's death. Failing health forced him to give up his post at Charterhouse and the story of his remaining life seems unhappily to have been one of sombre descent.

Cruel fate had struck yet again. The horror of his boy hurling himself in front of a train preyed upon a mind still haunted by the killing of William Foster and also anguished by the more recent death of his wife. It was more than enough to drive men to drink and, perhaps, he now sought too much solace in the bottle. He was a broken man.

Dogged by a diseased heart, financially insecure and later to be stricken by paralysis, Caesar 'gave up housekeeping and took up his abode' at the Railway Tavern in Mill Lane, Godalming. Occasionally, said the *West Surrey Times*, he ventured into public life 'to smoke a homely pipe or to have a quiet talk with his fellows, although he bore no resemblance of his former self, and it was evident to all who knew him that his time was well-nigh played out'.

Some fair-weather followers may have backed off, but true friends did what they could for the former cricket hero now in such straitened circumstances, and the esteem in which he was still held was reflected in 'many a quiet manner' during his illness. Frederick Marshall, the Surrey president, launched an appeal to aid the ailing man and, in an open letter that appeared in the December 8, 1877 issue of *Bell's Life*, he wrote:

I am sure that all lovers of cricket will be sorry to hear that Julius Caesar, the once renowned player of Surrey, is in the depths of poverty. Illness and family troubles have produced this state of things. He once had friends amongst all classes and all who remember him will acknowledge him to have been a plucky, straightforward, honest man, full of fun, yet always in his place. It will be an act of real kindness if his old friends will remember him now in the days of his decadence. Mr Alcock, the secretary of the Surrey club, has kindly undertaken to receive subscriptions which may be forwarded to him at the Surrey County Cricket Club Ground, Kennington Oval, London S.E. I have sent him a cheque for £10 for this good object.

The response was moderate, but it enabled Caesar to have a measure of those comforts and attention in his receding weeks that, as one admirer put it, 'an old favourite of the public has a fair right to expect'.

During the evening of Tuesday, March 5, 1878, just 20 days before his 48th birthday, Julius Caesar died. A local journalist, who would have known him well, had no doubt at all that the 'great sorrow caused by the suicide of his son some time ago played an active part in hastening his decline'.

Word of Caesar's end swept through the town. 'Lamentations are loud and general and indicate, to some extent, the loss entailed,' said the *Surrey Standard*. Another local reporter commented: 'Of his faults, if any, it becomes us not here to speak. As a cricketer, he was a bold, skilful and withal honest player all round, simply doing his best for the good of his club and ready on all occasions to uphold to the utmost of his powers the honour and dignity of the town and county that gave him birth. And now that the hand of death has stricken him down, there is no man who can raise his voice and say that he ever played it false.' *The Sporting Life* also praised Caesar as a fine cricketer, adding that a 'series of unlooked-for misfortunes, coupled with bad health and domestic affliction, broke up this once strong and jovial man'.

On March 11, Caesar's body, in an oak-boarded coffin draped with black cloth and topped by a few wreaths of 'choice spring flowers', was borne from the Railway Tavern by six of his closest friends. Following, in slow, measured tread, came a procession numbering about 40 and headed by his two surviving sons, Frederick and Charles Benjamin. The mourners moved silently past the church where Julius was baptised, over the river bridge and along Borough Road, beside the meadow to the parish cemetery in Nightingale Road almost a mile away. Before the cortege arrived there, some three or four hundred people, among them Surrey colleagues Harry Jupp and James Street, had assembled at the sloping burial ground. It was a worthy turn-out for Godalming's most renowned cricketer and 'many a tear was seen to fall from the eyes of stalwart-looking men'.

Shortly after three o'clock on that dull, rain-spotted Monday afternoon, the coffin was lowered gently into the freshly-dug soil and men and women shuffled past to pay their last respects before departing. Thus the 'remains of the once-famed Julius Caesar were laid to rest in their final abode on earth' – in the same plot as his beloved wife Jane, who had been buried there almost four years earlier. No headstone marked the spot, and it was not until the year 2000, after attention had several times been drawn to the sad

The Railway Tavern, next to Godalming railway station. Here Caesar lived out his final days of misery.

oversight, that the civic authorities in Godalming took the initiative and drew up plans to put a memorial in place 122 years after the great cricketer's death. A further step was taken in recognition of an unjustly forgotten man when Godalming Cricket Club promoted the idea of a Caesar Shield to be played for annually by the colts of Godalming and Farncombe.

What of those contemporaries of Caesar who, like him, expended their energy in their younger days on the cricket fields of England and elsewhere?

George Parr retired from the action in 1870 to live out his time in his native Radcliffe-on-Trent, later becoming a 'feeble and decrepit old man, his hair white, his form attenuated by sickness' before his death in 1891, aged 65. Richard Daft (64) survived his Nottinghamshire colleague by nine years. The frail figure of Tom Hayward battled against tuberculosis until July 1876, when he was 41 and could endure no more. His former batting partner, Bob Carpenter, lived to see 1901, during which year 'Foghorn' Jackson (68), of the 'fearful pace', also died – in the Liverpool Workhouse Infirmary.

Stout-hearted Tom Lockyer succumbed to consumption at the age of 43 just three days before Christmas 1869. The following May saw the end, in his mid-sixties, of Fuller Pilch, the one-time champion batsman. Jemmy Grundy (49), of the velvet cap, and graceful Joseph Guy (59) went in 1873, to be followed two years later by 'Mad Charlie' Brown (60) and F.P.Miller

(47), Surrey captain during memorable seasons. In 1876, George Brockwell died at 65, the much-loved Felix at 71, Tom Box at 68 and 'Ducky' Diver at 51. One by one, the immortals were shown to be mortal after all. Tom Nixon departed in 1877 in his 63rd year; Tom Humphrey, not yet 40, in 1878; Johnny Wisden at 57 in 1884. Other great players of Caesar's halcyon days lived on, none longer than William Caffyn. Not until 1919, in his 92nd year, did he concede defeat.

The influential Marshall family, who had been so supportive of Caesar, had also been depleted by death. Murray Marshall was 47 when he expired after a lingering illness in January 1870, preceding by 20 months his brother, Alexander, aged 51. Their mother, Sarah, widow of the timber merchant, George Marshall (died on Christmas Eve 1853), passed away on March 10, 1874 in her 77th year. Six months afterwards 79-year-old Henry Marshall, several times Mayor of Godalming and former president of Surrey CCC, died at his home in the High Street.

Henry's nephew, General Sir Frederick Marshall, who had followed him into that presidential office (1867-1879), was also devoted to cricket and the county club. An old campaigner of the Crimean and Zulu Wars, his upright military figure was a familiar sight at The Oval for many years before he breathed his last at the age of 70 on June 8, 1900. Colonel Harry Marshall, the last surviving brother, died at 81 just months before the Great War.

Broadwater House, once the home of the Marshalls, is no more. The lake still shimmers in the sunlight and weekend cricket continues to flourish nearby, where today's players tread turf alongside that once graced by the Godalming carpenter who, in the words of *The Times*, went 'grey in the pursuit of his favourite pastime'.

Julius Caesar, who typified the mid-19th century professional cricketer, proved himself as a top-class performer and few were better known or more loved during his sporting era. He contributed in no small measure to an important stage in the game's transition from comparative obscurity to widespread acceptance.

When he died, the so-called 'Golden Age' loomed a few years ahead to enrich the tapestry of cricket. It can justly be claimed that Julius Caesar was among its early prospectors.

PRINCIPAL SOURCES OF INFORMATION

A.A.Thomson, who wrote so agreeably about cricket, once observed with impish humour that to crib from a single book was plagiarism, to crib from a dozen amounted to research, and to crib from more might get you a doctorate of philosophy at one of the less-exacting universities. While entertaining no hope whatever of a PhD, the author of this book confesses to having 'cribbed' a little from each of the following:

BOOKS AND BOOKLETS:

Association of Cricket Statisticians: *Cricket Matches; First-Class Cricket Matches; Statistical Surveys; Surrey Cricketers 1839-1980*

Altham, H.S.: *A History of Cricket* [Allen & Unwin, 1926]

Alverstone, Lord and Alcock,C.W.: *Surrey Cricket: Its History and Associations* [Longmans, 1902]

Arrowsmith, R.L.: *A History of County Cricket: Kent* [Arthur Barker, 1971]

Brookes, Christopher: *English Cricket* [Weidenfeld & Nicholson, 1978]

Caffyn, William: *Seventy-One Not Out* [Blackwood, 1899]

Collyer, Graham: *Farnham Cricket Club 1782-1982* [Farnham Castle Newspapers, 1982]

Daft, Richard: *Kings of Cricket* [Arrowsmith, 1893]

Ford, John: *Cricket: A Social History 1700-1835* [David & Charles, 1972]

Frith, David: *The Fast Men* [Van Nostrand Reinhold, 1975]; *The Slow Men* [George Allen & Unwin, 1984]

Haygarth, Arthur: *Cricket Scores and Biographies* (volumes 1-11)

Janaway, John: *The Story of Godalming* [Local Heritage Books, 1983]

Kilburn, J.M.: *A History of Yorkshire Cricket* [Stanley Paul, 1970]

Lillywhite, Fred: *The English Cricketers' Trip to Canada and the United States in 1859* [first published in 1860; reprint with an introduction by Robin Marlar, World's Work, 1980]

Marshall, John: *Sussex Cricket* [Heinemann, 1959]

Morrah, Patrick: *Alfred Mynn and the Cricketers of His Time* [Eyre & Spottiswood, 1963]

Nyren, John: *The Cricketers of My Time* [first published,1833. Included in *From Hambledon to Lord's*, edited and introduced by John Arlott, Christopher Johnson, 1948]

Pycroft, James: *The Cricket Field* [Longmans, 1854]

Rait Kerr, R.S.: *The Laws of Cricket: Their History and Growth* [Longmans, 1950]

Ross, Gordon: *A History of County Cricket: Surrey* [Arthur Barker, 1971]

Thomson, A.A.: *Cricket: The Golden Ages* [Stanley Paul, 1961]

NEWSPAPERS:
Bell's Life in London; The Leader (Melbourne); *New York Herald; New York Times; Nottinghamshire Daily Guardian; Nottingham Journal; The Sporting Life; Surrey Advertiser; Surrey Gazette; Surrey Standard; Sydney Morning Herald; The Times; West Surrey Times; Sussex Express; Toronto Globe*

PARISH RECORDS:
Godalming: *Registers of Baptisms, Marriages and Burials* (c. 1816-1878)
Farncombe: *Registers of Baptisms and Marriages* (1850 and 1875)
Peper Harow: *Register of Baptisms* (1797)
Stoke-next-Guildford: *Register of Marriages* (1851)

GENERAL REGISTER OFFICE:
Certificates of births, deaths and marriages

CENSUS RETURNS:
Godalming (and Farncombe) and Guildford

INTERNATIONAL GENEALOGICAL INDEX

Julius Caesar's batting record in first-class (i.e. major) matches, as shown in *Who's Who of Cricketers* (Bailey, Thorn, Wynne-Thomas), is:
194 matches   333 innings   24 not-outs   4879 runs   average 15.78
3 centuries   highest score 132 not out   181 catches